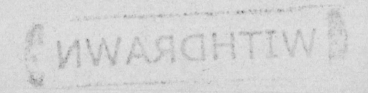

TWAYNE'S WORLD AUTHORS SERIES
A Survey of the World's Literature

CHINA

William Schultz, University of Arizona

EDITOR

P'i Jih-hsiu

TWAS 530

A nineteenth century woodblock
carving of Deer-Gate Mountain

P'I JIH-HSIU

By WILLIAM H. NIENHAUSER, JR.
University of Wisconsin

TWAYNE PUBLISHERS
A DIVISION OF G. K. HALL & CO., BOSTON

Printed on permanent/ durable acid-free paper and bound
in the United States of America

First Printing

Library of Congress Cataloging in Publication Data

Nienhauser, William H.
P'i Jih-hsiu.

(Twayne's world authors series ; TWAS 530)
Bibliography: p.
Includes index.
1. P'i, Jih-hsiu, ca. 834-ca. 883.   2. Poets,
Chinese—Biography.
PL2677.P5Z79   895.1'1'3 [B]   78-23230
ISBN 0-8057-6372-4

For Judith

um deretwillen
man reitet so spät durch Nacht und Wind

Contents

About the Author

William H. Nienhauser, Jr. was born in St. Louis, Missouri on December 10, 1943. He began his study of Chinese at the Army Language School in 1962, and took all three degrees at Indiana University (A.B., 1966; A.M., 1968; Ph. D., 1972). As a graduate student he spent a year at the University of Bonn (1967–68), and has since returned to the Federal Republic of Germany as an Alexander von Humboldt Foundation research fellow in 1975–76 (University of Hamburg) and 1977 (University of Munich). After serving as a Visiting Assistant Professor in the Department of Germanic Languages at Indiana University for one year (1972–73), he has been an Assistant Professor in the Department of East Asian Languages and Literature at the University of Wisconsin. He has published several books and articles on Chinese literature, including *Liu Tsung-yüan* (co-author) in the *Twayne World Author Series*, and is an editor of *Chinese Literature: Essays, Articles and Reviews*, a new journal which began publication in January 1979.

Preface

Most obviously this book is written to present P'i Jih-hsiu, a literatus of the ninth century, and his work to the English reader. At present there are very few translations of his writings available in English. Yet living in a time of social and intellectual change as he did, and reflecting this turmoil in bifurcated literary and official careers, his varied corpus has proved to be of interest to the Chinese reader, as is evident from the bibliography in the present volume. This study proposes to go a step further. Where Chinese scholars have extolled either one side or another of P'i's personality and writings (witness the divergent interpretations of his early didactic and later aesthetic pieces by his critics during the 1920s and 1930s), this volume intends to strike a more balanced view.

The late Etienne Balazs has noted that he hoped his studies of antiquity would not be without present-day relevance. In this spirit chapter 1 attempts to rearrange the rather limited biographical data on P'i according to four types of behavior patterns: innovation, rituality, retreat, and rebellion. Chapter 2 applies James J. Y. Liu's theories on the types of Chinese literary criticism to P'i's critical corpus, which is determined to be "pragmatic" during his early years, and "technical" later on. Through an examination of P'i's prose writings, chapter 3 concludes that "as a man from the periphery of the social groups which had defined and transmitted classical texts and knowledge for so long, his ideas are of significance in viewing the intellectual history of the important transitional era in which he lived." An explication of his poetry in chapter 4 gives strong evidence that "P'i is a very representative late T'ang poet," and that "the unfolding of his poetics encompasses both of the major schools of this era." The final chapter reviews the nature and reception of P'i's life and writings, showing how critics have biased their appreciation by considering only one aspect of his work, and concluding that they are likely to do so in the future.

Aside from stating my purposes in writing this book, there are certain methodological matters which should be clarified here. First, in discussing the rhythm of a work, "word" has been used to render *tzu*, although alternative translations such as "lexic" or "graph" may have been preferable, in order not to perplex the general reader. Second, in the translation of botanical terms, Tu Ya-ch'üan's *Chih-wu-hsüeh ta tz'u-tien* (A Dictionary of Botanical Terms, Taipei: Wen-kuang t'u-shu yu-hsien kung-ssu, 1971), which gives only Latin generic equivalents, and Liberty Hyde Bailey's *Hortus Third: A Concise Dictionary of Plants Cultivated in the United States and Canada* (New York: Macmillan Company, 1976), which is arranged according to these generic labels, have been the most important aids. Third, on occasion I have made little explanation of certain official titles mentioned in the text. Yet we should remember that any bureaucracy, including that of the T'ang dynasty, functions smoothly only on paper, and that more valuable information concerning an official position can usually be found in the writings of someone who had occupied it than in the various theoretic or idealized statements of traditional reference works. Finally, I should like to note that translated titles are given in parentheses when they are established renderings, and in brackets when they are my translation.

Mention is traditionally made in this format to mentors, colleagues, and others who have helped in the preparations of the manuscript. To Professor Irving Yucheng Lo I owe a capacious debt. From the time he introduced me to P'i Jih-hsiu through the gift of Teng T'o's *Hsin-pien T'ang-shih san-pai-shou* half a dozen years ago, he has steadfastly supported and aided my work. Aside from providing me a sounding board for some of my ideas, he has corrected numerous errors in translations and judgment. Since coming to the University of Wisconsin nearly five years ago, I have presented P'i's poems in an informal poetry-reading group within the Department of East Asian Languages and Literature several times. The comments of my colleagues, especially those of Professors Tse-tsung Chow, Tsai-fa Cheng, and Francis Westbrook, and the often equally rewarding suggestions of many of our graduate students, have been invaluable. Four students deserve special mention. Professor Dennis T. Hu, now a visiting member of the faculty of the Department of East Asian Languages and Literature, University of Oregon, served as my project assistant during the summer of 1977 and helped especially with the first chapter. Mr. Karl S. Y. Kao has read the entire manuscript, prevented countless infelicities, and finally come to appreciate P'i's style. Ms. Jane P. Yang served as my project assistant during the first semester of the 1977–78 academic year; she, too, has read and revised numerous passages, typed and re-

Preface

typed the manuscript, and been a ready listener. Thanks are also due Ms. Sharon Shih-jiuan Hou, my current project assistant, who has especially enhanced the quality of the scholarship and the translations. Mr. Ching-lin Wang worked through a number of poems with me during the initial stages of my research. Professor Michael B. Fish of the University of Oregon has taken time from a particularly busy year to read the entire manuscript and offer me suggestions which have strengthened this study and deepened my understanding of the late T'ang era in general.

I wish to express as well my appreciation and debt to the Graduate School of the University of Wisconsin, which has underwritten some of the research for this volume and provided me with project assistants. Alexander von Humboldt Foundation support afforded me the stimulating environment of the University of Munich for the summer of 1977 when I began writing. My academic mentor in Munich, Professor Herbert Franke, proved the ideal model of someone who has studied the traditional and yet remains very much a viable part of today; my thanks to him and to his staff at the Institut für Ostasienkunde for their inspiration and cordiality. Professor T. H. Tsien of the Far Eastern Library, University of Chicago, and Professor Chester Wang of the Memorial Library, University of Wisconsin, have provided various texts and valuable advice. And I am grateful to Professor Joseph S. M. Lau, who has patiently encouraged and exhorted me throughout this project. Naturally I can thank only myself for the errors which remain.

It is difficult to express the gratitude I feel to my son, Daniel, and my daughter, Susan, for their moral and practical support. Both have shuffled note cards, briefcases, and themselves according to my moods, particularly during the last few months. In partial repayment for the understanding, friendship, and devotion of my wife, Judith, this volume is dedicated to her.

Finally, I should like to cite a comment by René Girard: "The critical act cannot be immediate. Rather it has to span the whole distance between fascination and the opposite which we call explication."[1] Since the explication in this volume is but a taste of the life and writings of P'i Jih-hsiu and his contemporaries, it is my hope that many of the readers of this book will return to the fascination of P'i's original corpus.

WILLIAM H. NIENHAUSER, JR.

University of Wisconsin

Acknowledgments

To Doubleday and Company, Inc. for permission to reprint my translations of several of P'i Jih-hsiu's poems from *Sunflower Splendor*, © 1975 by Wu-chi Liu and Irving Yucheng Lo.

Chronology

ca. 834   P'i Jih-hsiu born in Hsiang-chou (modern Hsiang-yang, Hupei).
850s   Withdraws to Deer-Gate Mountain.
863–965   Tour through the Yangtze Valley in search of a patron.
866   Took *chin-shih* examination and failed. Retired to Shou-chou (modern Shou County, Anhwei) and compiled *P'i-tzu wen-sou*.
867   Passed *chin-shih* examination.
868   Took *Po-hsüeh hung-tz'u* examination and failed. Left later in the year apparently for Shou-chou, but detoured to Soochow to avoid an uprising.
869   Arrived in Soochow. Was given a minor post under the prefect, Ts'ui P'u, and met Lu Kuei-meng.
871   Wrote preface to *Sung-ling chi*, a collection compiled by Lu Kuei-meng containing the poetry P'i and Lu wrote together primarily during 870.
early 870s Married (for the second time?).
872   Followed Ts'ui P'u to a post in T'ung-chou (modern Ta-li County in Shensi).
874–875   Returned to Soochow.
877   In Ch'ang-an as Adjunct Secretary in Charge of Redaction and Professor at the National University. First Son, P'i Kuang-yeh, born.
878–879   Second son, P'i Kuang-lin, born.
880   Made Deputy Commissioner of P'i-ling in Ch'ang-chou (modern Wu-chin County, Kiangsu), but encountered Huang Ch'ao's army en route and joined them.
881–883   Served Huang Ch'ao's Ch'i Dynasty as Han-lin Academician in Ch'ang-an.
ca. 883   Died, probably executed by Huang Ch'ao.

CHAPTER 1

Patterns of Disaster:
Life and Times

I Social and Political Backgrounds

NIETZSCHE has argued that "the little force which is necessary to shove a skiff into the stream should not be confused with the force of this stream, which carries it further: but it happens in almost every biography."[1] Despite this sagacious admonition, it is essential to begin this study with an examination of the streams through which P'i Jih-hsiu (*ca.* 834-*ca.* 883) directed his skiff.

The history of the late T'ang is represented in many ways by the years 833-835, those of the thirteenth through sixteenth of the rule of Wen-tsung (r. 827–840),[2] fourteenth emperor of the T'ang dynasty. In Ssu-ma Kuang's (1019–1086) account of this period in his *Tzu-chih t'ung-chien* [Comprehensive Mirror for Aid in Government],[3] there are the following items of interest:

1) In the second (lunar) month of 833 Li Te-yü (787–850) was made a chief minister and summoned by the emperor to discuss the problem of factional rivalry dominating political life.

Ironically, Li was the head of one of the two primary cabals (the other headed by Niu Seng-ju [779–847]).[4] The feud lasted from 808 until nearly 860, when the leaders finally passed from the scene. It was truly one of the major problems of Wen-tsung's reign.[5]

2) In the fourth month the Uighurs took a new khan.

This was Prince Hu,[6] and although he and his people played only a very tangential role in the T'ang politics of this period, they had been earlier the most important Central Asian T'ang ally. Thus this event holds an ominous significance for the increasingly vital role

15

which foreign armies were to play in the turmoil of the ninth century.

3) In the sixth month the Military Governor of Western Shan-nan Province (centering about the area where the borders of the modern provinces of Szechwan, Kansu, and Shensi meet), Li Tsai-i (788–837),[7] was made Military Governor of Ho-tung (the northern parts of modern Shansi and Hopei).

The increasing reliance of the T'ang throne on military governors had been a constant concern of the central government since the mid-eighth century. By the mid-ninth century these provincial bases of power were too well established to be threatened by anything the court might have wished to undertake.

4) In the seventh month Li Te-yü suggested that the *chin-shih* (presented scholar) national civil service examinations be made more practical by de-emphasizing their belletristic aspects.

Such appeals became more and more widespread during the late T'ang period,[8] both from those segments of society which owed their rise to power and preeminence to the examination system, and from those members of the aristocracy, many of whom had argued that the examinations served only to determine who was blessed with a good memory. In short, the awareness of contemporary literati and bureaucrats that the examination system was a potential force in shaping the political and social structures of the ninth century can be seen in this passage.

5)-In the twelfth month, after the emperor had suffered a stroke, he was left unable to speak. Wang Shou-ch'eng (d. 835), the powerful eunuch, recommended Cheng Chu (d. 835), a minor official with some medical knowledge, to administer to him. In the first month of 834, the emperor's condition improved and as a result Cheng Chu found great imperial favor. In the sixth month the emperor called for proposals to bring about an end to the drought. Li Chung-min (fl. 820–835) memorialized, urging the recall of Sung Shen-hsi (d. 833[9]), an adamant opponent of the eunuchs who was then in disgrace, and calling as well for the execution of Cheng Chu. In the tenth month of 835 Cheng Chu had Wang Shou-ch'eng murdered. During the eleventh month a plot to assassinate many of the eunuchs failed, and in retaliation hundreds of officials were put to death.

These passages speak to another of the nemeses of the ninth-century T'ang government. This particular chain of events led to the Sweet Dew Incident,[10] which was the most vigorous attempt ever aimed at the elimination of the eunuchs in a single coup de grace. Its failure left the T'ang court even more in the hands of the eunuchs.

6) In the seventh month of 835 the Tzu-yün Lou (Purple Cloud Pavilion) was built on the Ch'ü-chiang (Winding River) in southeast Ch'ang-an.

This observation by Ssu-ma Kuang may be intended to suggest the growing attention paid to ceremonies and all manners of festivals by the rulers of the late T'ang. The Winding River was a favorite site for such gatherings.

7) In the second month of 834 there was an eclipse.

Perhaps such a record of a natural omen[11] best typifies the latter part of the ninth century, for the era was indeed one of eclipse marked by the collapse of political and social orders which had stood for centuries.

During this same three-year period P'i Jih-hsiu was born. The problems depicted above—factionalism, Central Asian military dominance, decentralization of economic and political power, the increasing deterioration of the civil service examinations, the gradual usurpation of many of the bureaucracy's rights and powers by the eunuchs, and the malaise, both physical and psychic, surrounding the royal family—plagued most of the T'ang rulers from 820 on. During the reigns of the three emperors under whom P'i's adult years were spent—Hsüan-tsung (r. 847–859), I-tsung (r. 860–873), and Hsi-tsung (r. 874–888)[12]—these administrative and moral cancers ran rampant, leaving the T'ang rulers little more than a pretense to power after the suppression of the Huang Ch'ao Rebellion and P'i's death in the early 880s.

Yet this negative process made way for the chiliastic upheavals of the Sung dynasty (960–1279).[13] Prodded by incessant warfare in the Yellow River valley, and attracted to the agriculturally advanced and prosperous lower Yangtze valley, millions moved south and east during the ninth century. The resultant breakdown of the old conscript military system, based upon a sedentary, carefully registered population, along with the ever-increasing power of the provincial "warlords," led to the formation of professional armies and eventu-

ally to a redefinition of the concept of the son of heaven—the emperor—who was no longer an aristocratic *primus inter pares,* but,
especially from the Sung on, an autocrat who acquired and maintained his position through a nucleus of elite, loyal troops. The
hegira southward also dictated changes in land ownership and taxa-
tion. Yang Yen's (727–781) reforms of 780 eventually reinforced the
concept of private ownership of land and led to the rise of manors
and landlords. Moreover, China's economy changed in accord with
the other transformations of demographic and military potential.
Tea, and especially salt, both products of the lower Yangtze region,
provided much of the government's annual revenue.[14] The com-
merce involved in the production, shipment, and distribution of
these products was gradually turned over to merchants, since official
provincial channels were no longer considered reliable. This em-
bryonic interregional trading fostered the growth of cities, particularly in the Southeast.

As landlords, rich peasants, provincial small-gentry clans, and
merchants undermined the traditional social strata, the oligarchy,
which had in essence ruled since the Han dynasty (206 B.C.–A.D.
220), crumbled, making way for these "new men." And these social
changes began to be reflected in T'ang culture and literature.

II *The Cultural and Literary Backgrounds*

Beginning with the Ta-li reign period (766–779) there was a tendency to reject traditional exegeses of the classics.[15] A related
movement, the *ku-wen* or "neoclassical" movement, saw a return to
the ideas and styles of these works themselves. All of this was
perhaps a legacy of Liu Chih-chi (661–721), who in his magnum
opus, the *Shih-t'ung* (Study of Historiography), set historiographic
standards, which led not only to a reevaluation of the classics, but
also to the production of the first consciously fictional genre, the
ch'uan-ch'i.[16] In some ways this attention to the past was a type of
proto-nationalism, a reaction to the strong foreign influences of the
T'ang dynasty. After over a century of expansion (from approximately 620 to 750), moreover, the marches had become potential
trouble spots. The Tibetans, Nan-chao (a Thai kingdom located in
modern Yunnan), the Turks, and the Koreans all grew more daring
in their relations with T'ang. Arab traders were also seen as a
menace.[17] Indeed, even the hated eunuchs were perhaps viewed as

"foreign," since many of them came from peripheral regions or minority peoples.

But whatever the cause,[18] *ku-wen* scholars began to return to the Han and even to the Chou for models before the "barbarian" had first made his presence felt. Led by *Spring and Autumn Annals* (Ch'un-ch'iu) specialists, who because of inconsistencies between the (Tso Commentary) *Tso chuan* and this classic began to reinterpret the *Spring and Autumn Annals* itself, they rejected all intermittent exegesis and advocated a return to the classics. This skepticism was widespread among such literati. Examples of this *Zeitgeist* include: Liu Tsung-yüan's (773–819)[19] attacks on the authorship or authenticity of many supposed "classics";[20] Lai Ku's (d. *ca.* 881)[21] advocacy of the wisdom of village elders over the tradition of the *Book of Rites* (Li-chi);[22] and Ch'eng Yen's (fl. *ca.* 900)[23] "discovery," in a fictionalized interview[24] with Mao Yen-shou (the artist traditionally condemned for misrepresenting Wang Chao-chün's beauty),[25] that the painter was moved by patriotic feelings (he did not want the emperor to become infatuated with Wang).

Much of this is no doubt attributable to the social changes of this era. Many of these literati belonged to families which were just emerging (or reemerging after a long period of dormancy) in the higher strata of society. Sociologists maintain that the stress produced by such changes produces one of four types of behavior: innovation, rituality, retreat, or rebellion.[26] Conformity, as a standard, is often defined as the adaptation to cultural goals and to the institutionalized means to reach them. Innovation means maintenance of goals to be reached by new means. Rituality is the adherence to the standard means, concurrent with the creation of new goals. Retreat is marked by a rejection of both goals and means. And rebellion reflects a completely new set of goals and procedures which the rebel seeks to institutionalize.

Although some literati chose conformity or rituality, many who lived during the brouhaha of the ninth century were innovators. Their desire was to reform the means of achieving the traditional goals of the scholar-official. This necessitated a change in the procedures and content of the examinations (such as Li Te-yü was seeking), some extraofficial means of communication with the sovereign (since official lines had come under eunuch control), and, even more basically, a simplification of the language involved in these communications (such as that advocated by the *ku-wen* supporters).

These socio-cultural trends are reflected in late T'ang literature.
It was a period which today, with the literary-historiographic
hindsight of over a millenium, must be considered innovative. New
genres such as the lyric *(tz'u)*,[27] the *pien-wen* (a Buddhist-
influenced form of narrative written in a colloquial style of alter-
nated prose and verse), the *ch'uan-ch'i* (classical-language tale), and
the *Hsin Yüeh-fu*[28] (New Music Bureau verse, didactic and socially
critical poems in which the government was denounced, often by
peasant personae) were popular. These new forms represented a
trend away from euphuism and elitism, and a de-emphasis of canonical works which had been virtually memorized by a small group
of literati, toward a much more catholic, in all senses of the word,
corpus attended by a larger, but less well-read, readership. By Sung
times readers turned to commentaries for that which their precur-
sors had understood easily. The emphasis which the Buddhists at-
tached to popularization, vis-à-vis Confucian neglect, helped force
the latter to a more eclectic stance, and eventually toward that
compromise known today as Neo-Confucianism.

Yet the conventional, the ritualized, the anchoritic, and the rebellious were also present. Classical-language essays, traditional
poetry (the *shih*), prose-poems (or *fu*, written primarily in preparation for the examinations), and even the euphuistic *p'ien-wen*
(parallel-prose) style still enjoyed a large following (the latter especially at court, as official documents continued to be written in this
vacuous, florid style) and may be considered to represent the conventional or the ritualized.

Generally, however, one can trace three schools of late T'ang
poetry.[29] The first, often said to have begun with Po Chü-i (772–
846), and seen in its purest form in the angrier tones of Tu Hsün-ho
(846–904), Nieh I-chung (837–*ca.* 889), and Lo Yin (833–909),[30]
exhibits a social concern and a starkly simple diction. It may be seen
especially in the New Music Bureau verse, which Po invented and
to a great degree helped to popularize; it represented an attempt to
reach the court through extraofficial, albeit traditional, means. The
second, an aesthetic school which took the baroque style of Li
Shang-yin (813–858) as its model, reflects the attitude of both re-
treatists and ritualists. It must be considered a natural development
from the frustrations of those who despaired of poetry's role to reach
and to move the large audience Po Chü-i had hoped for. Since those
individuals who should have paid Po's social commentaries heed did

not, these aesthetes felt no need to write for anyone except close friends or colleagues. The third group is a bifurcated school, perhaps intended as a "catchall" for all intermediates who neither espoused Po's commitment nor shared Li's pessimism. Chia Tao (779–849) and Chang Chi (766–829) are accounted the chief stylists of the two wings of this group.

III   *Growing Up in Hsiang-chou*

P'i Jih-hsiu[31] was born during or shortly after the year 833—probably in 834.[32] As with most Chinese literati of the time, little is known of his youth. He was born in Hsiang-chou (modern Hsiang-yang in Hupei Province), a provincial capital in one of the more populous regions in the empire—the entire prefecture had a population of around 550,000 at that time.[33] The city was one of the most important T'ang commercial centers[34] and was renowned for its lacquer ware.[35] Located on the Han River, it marked a layover for many emigrants heading south from the capital. The area also enjoyed a literary reputation, boasting Tu Fu (712–770) and Meng Hao-jan (689–740) among its native sons. Though few details about the P'i clan are available, some particulars of the milieu in which P'i grew up can be ascertained. His childhood was probably spent in the countryside around the prefectural seat. His literary corpus reflects a rural setting, perhaps a modest compound near Ching-ling (modern T'ien-men County), located in Hupei just north of the watersmeet of the Han and Yangtze rivers.

During P'i's childhood the area was relatively free of major disturbances. There were, however, frequent floods during the mid-830s.[36] His family, despite the claims of various scholars in the People's Republic, were most probably not peasants. According to a genealogy P'i wrote himself,[37] they were descended from a long, noble ancestry. P'i Ch'u had been Governor of Hsiang-yang during the Tsin dynasty (265–419)[38] and P'i Ching-ho (521–575) was enfeoffed as a prince during the Northern Ch'i dynasty (550–588).[39] But during Sui (589–618) and T'ang times the P'is lost much of their social status, and no one had been able to reestablish it through success in the examinations. They subsisted by farming fields near Ching-ling or by living as recluses, for after P'i's great-uncle, P'i Hang-hsiu,[40] no one in the clan had held even a minor position. There is, moreover, certain evidence in support of the idea that P'i's family held the status of *wang-tsu:* a locally prominent clan, but one

which could not attain high office in the central government or
attract the attention of the court-based historians.[41] After P'i had
failed in his attempt to become a *chin-shih* (presented scholar, i.e.,
an examination graduate) in 866, for example, he retired to a country villa to edit his writings.[42] Although this estate may have been
provided by a patron, it would have been highly unusual for a
member of the T'ang aristocracy to support a peasant. Moreover, P'i
wrote a poem "seeing off" a younger cousin, P'i Ch'ung, who was
returning to Fu-chou (modern Mien-yang County in Hupei).[43] Such
mobility would be out of the question for a peasant family. And of
course there is P'i's literary talent, his hubris, and his predilection
for wine, characteristics on which all of his various biographers concur, which are not likely the result of a peasant upbringing. They
correspond more closely to the mores of the scholar-official class.[44]

Though this study is not sociological or psychological in orientation, it may be of benefit to consult both of these social sciences in
dealing with P'i's life. For the milieu of the ninth century was one of
change, and this is one of the central problems of sociology.[45] The
general improvement of P'i's own social position may explain some
of his character traits. Moreover, if one accepts the four major stages
of social change postulated by Robert A. Nisbet, 1) impetus, 2)
means of transmission of this impetus throughout the social structure, 3) alternations of authority relationship and social roles within
the structure, and 4) the complex psychological modifications of
individual life organizations to new roles and relationships, i.e., the
strains and tensions bound up in the crisis of change,[46] one will be
forced to consider the psychological framework of the life of a man
such as P'i Jih-hsiu who experienced so much change. Although the
data available on P'i's youth is too meager to model our study on
Erik Erikson's work, nevertheless Erikson's conclusions that there
are psychological stages of life beyond childhood[47] may be of use in
helping to explain the drastic vacillation of P'i's life.

The outstanding event of P'i's youth (at least for the concerns of
this study) was his retirement to the hermitage of Deer-Gate Mountain (Lu-men Shan), a retreat located on the east bank of the Han
River southeast of Hsiang-yang[48] where Meng Hao-jan also so-
journed. How long P'i spent in this aerie is unknown, but one may
speculate that the time was intended to be employed preparing for
the examinations. The following poem captures one aspect of his life
at Deer-Gate:

A Summer's Day at Deer-Gate

The courtyard filled with pine and cassia shadow,
It's noon, but you wouldn't know it.
The man of the mountain suddenly awakes,
The magpie before the hall still hasn't moved.
Out from under the eaves he follows the clouds' departure,
Forgetting to put on his white hat.[49]
About to write, his eyes seem to have thin mists before them,
The wine in his bowels like water in a clepsydra.[50]
For those who strive for what lies beyond this life,
Drink and food are still necessary for support.
Then why not just stop eating,
And truly make oneself nonactive?[51]

Despite anecdotes depicting P'i's bibulousness[52] and despite the
tongue-in-cheek Taoist sentiments of this piece, which may be little
more than the formulaic utterance expected of a resident of Deer-
Gate, the poem translated below, which is also of this period, at
least serves as a foil to illustrate the contradictions of P'i's youth:

Reading

What sort of thing is our family wealth?
Piles of books arrayed up to the rafters.
At dawn in my lofty study I open a scroll,
And alone share in the words of the sages.
Though the superior and wise lived in another age,
Since ancient times they have approved of this frame of mind.
But these bookworms I see on my desk,
Still surpass one's ordinary companions.[53]

This verse adds to the evidence against P'i's peasant background. It
suggests the traditional literati attitude toward books. It also reveals
the haughtiness and arrogance which plagued P'i throughout his life
and may have led to his demise. In the third couplet, therefore, one
is tempted to insert a "we," for P'i certainly feels kindred to the
unrecognized sages of old. His disaffection with and disdain for his
contemporaries, seen in the final line, is another leitmotiv of P'i's
life.

Evidence that P'i was an avid reader is seen throughout his corpus. His gradually worsening vision (cf. the "thin mists before
them" of "A Summer's Day . . .") seems already at this early age to

have shown the strain of long hours of study. Secular provincial instruction at this time was primarily oriented toward providing a sort of moral tutelage, and not at all intended for those students aspiring for success in the bureaucracy.[54] These latter scholars studied with private teachers who were often chaired in retreats like Deer-Gate.[55] The curriculum was certainly based upon that of the *Kuo-tzu Chien* (The National University), involving the study of the *Book of Rites,* the *Spring and Autumn Annals* and its commentaries, the *Book of Poetry* (Shih-ching), the *Book of Changes* (I-ching), the *Book of Documents* (Shu-ching), the *Analects of Confucius* (Lun-yü, hereafter, cited as *Analects*), and the *Book of Filial Obedience* (Hsiao-ching).[56] Instruction in Deer-Gate no doubt included the study of belletristic works of local luminaries such as Tu Fu and Meng Hao-jan. The *Wen-hsüan,* long the handbook which might be studied in preparation for the examinations, seems to have been less influential at this time.[57] P'i's early writings reflect more of a pre-dilection for the socially committed writers of the generations immediately preceding him, especially Po Chü-i and Han Yü (768–824), as well as an interest in the *Songs of the South* (Ch'u-tz'u), normally the scriptures of those who chose to withdraw from the world.

P'i Jih-hsiu's literary vacillation suggests he spent some unsettling years pondering his future while at Deer-Gate. On the one hand, as he shows in his clan genealogy, he felt obligated to pursue an official career. His intellectual values, however, argued against such a course.[58] Even if he were to acquire the knowledge and literary skills requisite for success in the examinations and a resultant official career, there is evidence that already at this early point in his life P'i was disillusioned with the central government and skeptical concerning the possibilities of a career therein:

Mosquitoes[59]

Buzzing together like thunder,
They bite into flesh and know not surfeit.
As if something were amiss in high Heaven,
These little things are allowed to eat meat!
A poor scholar has no crimson gauze curtains,
He bears his misery lying in a thatched hut;
Why do they search here for the sleek and fat?
In this belly there's naught from the government granary![60]

The implication of this poem is that mosquitoes were better fed than the common people (line 4). The gauze curtains of line 5 are not mosquito netting, but the hangings which separated the eccentric scholar Ma Jung (79–166), who sat with his women on one side, from his students, who sat on the other.[61] It may be that P'i's satirical "Writings of a Recluse at Deer-Gate" (Lu-men yin-shu), a very secular collection of sixty pasquinades in which the government is truculently attacked, is also a work of this era.[62]

The following poem perhaps pictures the young man after having pursued both his avocations—wine and literature—on a single evening:

Sobering Up After an Idle Night

Awakening to the moon high above the mountains,
A single pillow midst a pile of books.
A thirst that listlessly turns from wine to tea,
But that mountain lad cannot be awakened.[63]

The boy supposed to be attending P'i is yet another sign of his elevated social status. The relaxed tone of the poem contains none of the conflict sensed elsewhere. This may be explained by the form (five-word-line poetry is by convention less tense than seven-word) and by the subject of the poem. Yet P'i clearly still had faith that the government could be reformed and the empire ruled in peace. This is nowhere revealed better than in a preface to P'i's series "Seven Beloved":

Master P'i's ambition is always to cherish truthfulness to oneself and simplicity.[64] Those who establish great governments must have true chancellors in their employ—I have taken Fang [Hsüan-ling, 578–648][65] and Tu [Ju-hui, 585–630][66] as my chancellors; those who have settled great disorders, must have a true general—I have taken Li Ta-wei [Li Sheng][67] as my true general; those who have contemned great lords must have a true recluse among them—I have taken Lu Cheng-chün [Lu Hung][68] as my true recluse; those who have repressed frivolous customs must have a true government servant—I have taken Yüan Lu-shan [Yüan Te-hsiu][69] as my true government servant; those who have borne up under an anchoritic temperament must have a true free spirit—I have taken Li Han-lin [Li Po][70] as my true free spirit; those who have become famous officials must have a true genius—I have taken Po the Grand Tutor [Po Chü-i][71] as my true genius . . .[72]

In this political *Weltanschauung* one sees simultaneously the internal conflict between active participation in the established political
order (Fang Hsüan-ling and Tu Ju-hui) and withdrawal from or
transcendence of it (Lu Hung and Li Po) that P'i felt during his years
at Deer-Gate. Again P'i reaches into the past for his models (cf.
"Reading," above). To some extent the world P'i desired was utopian, and thus his attempts to attain it were inevitably to be frustrated. Yet his concerns (moral influence, reclusive life, etc.) are
those of a man who has stepped back for a better perspective, but
who has not abandoned mankind.

In the second lunar month of 863 P'i demonstrated again his
concern by sending a memorial to the emperor in which he called
for the text of *Mencius* (Meng-tzu) to be added to that corpus of
material used in the national examinations.[73] Indeed, *Mencius* had
been considered an important, albeit neglected, text since Han Yü
praised it.[74] P'i's "Yüan p'ang" [On the Origin of Slander] and "Yüan
hua" [On the Origin of Moral Influence][75] both incorporate
many Mencian ideas, especially the concept that people have the
right to revolt if a country is ruled improperly.

At this time P'i was about thirty years old, and he had apparently
resolved, at least temporarily, any doubts he may have had concerning a career as an official. His studies completed (no doubt
including a thorough knowledge of *Mencius* in addition to the normal curriculum), he now set out to make contact with a provincial
official or satrap who might then use his influence to improve P'i's
chances in the examination and any subsequent career. He headed
thus not for the political capital at Ch'ang-an, but into the economic
heartland along the Yangtze basin where his family perhaps had
some connections (his cousin apparently lived in Fu-chou). En route
southward he paid a courtesy call on Cheng Ch'eng, the prefect of
Ying-chou (modern Chung-hsiang County), which was the nearest
administrative seat on the Han River and was probably the site of
some of the P'i clan's lands.[76] During the fourth month of 863 he
wrote a record *(chi)* of a temple there for Cheng.[77] For the next year
he wandered in the Yangtze region visiting old friends (such as Li
Chung-po)[78] and attempting to make new ones. Yet the journey was
not marked by amenities. This was due in part to P'i's importunate,
forward behavior, as the following anecdote illustrates:

P'i Jih-hsiu of the T'ang once paid a call on Kuei Jen-shao. Several times he went to him, but wasn't able to see him. P'i then became enraged and his arousal took form in words. Thus he wrote the "Ode on a Turtle" [the word for turtle was a homonym for the surname of the addressee, Mr. Kuei]:

> How many years have that solid frame and
>   useless body known?
> How could such a skeleton claim to
>   be a gallant?
> The obstinate skin will be perforated
>   to be used in divination after his passing;
> All because he's never stuck out
>   his head in his whole life.[79]

This sort of behavior notwithstanding, P'i claims he covered some six thousand miles and visited over a dozen prominent provincial figures during this trip.[80] Finally in early 865 he turned toward the capital, traveling through Nan-yang (modern Nan-yang County in Honan Province) and Shan-chou (modern Shan-chou County in Honan on the Yellow River) and arriving in the capital too late to take the examinations that year.

IV   Life in the Capital

Whether P'i's precipitate decision to leave the South and go to Ch'ang-an to take the examinations was the result of finding a patron is impossible to determine. Yet, in the preface to an inscription written as P'i entered the Lan-t'ien Pass near Ch'ang-an, he claims that "he was entering the capital aided by the recommendations of the feudal lords as a provincial candidate."[81] Whatever his credentials, he failed the examinations in 866 and retired to a villa in Shou-chou (modern Shou-chou County in Anhwei), which he had visited earlier in 864, to compile his *P'i-tzu wen-sou* [Literary Marsh of Master P'i; hereafter *Literary Marsh*], which he hoped would serve as a *hsing-chüan* (a collection of writings to be circulated among possible patrons, examiners, etc. by an examination candidate).[82] The villa, in addition to the costly expenses of preparing for the examinations and celebrating their completion, may have been contributed by a patron. These costs were especially heavy during the 860s when the processions and galas associated with the examinations became particularly extravagant and fines were imposed upon anyone who did not attend them.[83] Wei Chuang's (836–910)

"The Hsien-t'ung Reign Period [860–873]" looks back upon the
carpe diem spirit of this era:

> In the Hsien-t'ung period the general mentality ran to
>   the excess,
> As intensely joyous as the days of the houses of Chin,
>   Chang, Hsü and Shih;
> Though bankrupt, people struggled to retain the pleasures
>   of heaven,
> Casting mountains into cash in an attempt to buy blossoms
>   from the grotto.
> Silver lanterns converge after feasts of prominent gentlemen—
> Sylphs returning from pleasure jaunts as the jade moon sets.
> They seemed to sense how things would be today,
> And frantically piped and strummed as they sent those years
>   off.[84]

This poem was written sometime after the Hsien-t'ung era and depicts the hedonism of a generation which began to sense the demise
of the T'ang. There are several allusions to events of the Former
Han dynasty (206 B.C.–A.D. 9). Chin and Chang, in line 2, refer to
Chin Mi-ti (d. 86 B.C.) and Chang An-shih (d. 62 B.C.). They are
mentioned synecdochically to indicate those members of the "old"
families long in favor with the imperial family. Hsü and Shih in the
same line were coeval families with marriage ties to the Han throne.
This quartet collectively seems to refer to all those close to the
emperor, and to the excesses of I-tsung's court. There is in addition
some suggestion of misgovernment, since these families were powerful as a result of factionalism and favoritism. The phrase "casting
mountains into cash" alludes to Liu P'i's (213–154 B.C.) biography in
the *Shih-chi* (Records of the Grand Historian).[85] As King of Wu he
minted cash from the mountains and boiled sea water to obtain salt.
As a result, his kingdom prospered. But the other side of the allusive coin is just as apt here, for Wei Chuang intimates the unrest of
the 860s in calling Liu P'i to mind, since he was also the leader of the
Revolt of the Kings in 154 B.C. The grotto of line 4 is either that
which led to the utopia of T'ao Ch'ien's (*ca*. 372–427) "T'ao-hua yüan
chi" (Record of Peach-blossom Spring) or the *tzu-tung* (purple
grotto) where Lao-tzu is reputed to have eaten peaches which con-
ferred immortality.[86] In other words, the people of this Hsien-t'ung

decade pursued actual (elixirs and drugs) and metaphoric (pleasure) means to seek a utopian immortality.

Since P'i had neither the financial backing nor the social standing to allow him access to such revelry, it is possible that his presence in the capital was only effected through the patronage of a powerful and old aristocratic family. Such a family could have been that of Ling-hu T'ao (*ca.* 803–880), whom P'i visited when the former was Military Governor of Huai-nan Province in 866.[87] With or without Ling-hu's support, P'i passed the following year. Although his success is often attributed to the virtues of the *Literary Marsh* itself,[88] this seems unlikely, for this congeries of P'i's early satirical and critical pieces is similar to Lo Yin's *Ch'an-shu* [Book of Slander] written in 867, which supposedly prevented Lo Yin from ever passing the examinations.[89] Moreover, P'i passed near the bottom of the list and may have attained even this only by virtue of his unusual surname.[90] As a result, a fellow graduate and a member of the old aristocracy, Ts'ui Chao-fu,[91] and P'i's examiner himself, Cheng Yü, ridiculed him.[92] P'i was on better terms, however, with other graduates such as Wei Ch'eng-i and Sung K'ou;[93] he even directed a poem to the latter:

> Sent to Fellow Graduate Sung Ch'ui-wen,
> the Recorder,[94] on the Occasion of a Party in
> The Apricot Garden at Cold Food Festival Time After
> Having Passed the Examinations

Rain washes Pure and Clear, the myriad images are fresh;
Horses and carriages all over the city crowd to feasts
   in crimson banquet halls.
Favor and glory are mine as a companion to this lofty
   gathering.
Yet on account of the taboos of the examinations I
   worry that I might have offended the immortals.
Faced with wine I didn't sense it was "fire-lighting day";
As I am poor, how can this compare to the time we spent
   looking at flowers?
Though here I fear to be mocked by some beauty's smile,
Since I've not yet paid for this one feast midst the
   spring breezes.[95]

Playing the literal meaning of pure and clear against the spring festival of the same name, P'i begins the description of this post-examination party. Line 2 refers to the trappings every graduate was required to display in these celebrations (see note 83 above). But the tone of the poem marks a return to P'i's ambivalence with regard to an official career. In the second couplet he seems concerned that his success came at the cost of losing favor with important members of the court, perhaps his examiner. His imbibing may be that referred to in the anecdote concerning Ts'ui Chao-fu.[96] The fire-lighting day is the sort of spring holiday known in many cultures. It follows the Clear and Pure Festival, when only cold food is eaten and the "winter fires" are extinguished.[97] Flower viewing refers on the surface to excursions midst the apricot blossoms along the Winding River and to this traditional post examination gathering. It indicates further the courtesans (euphemistically termed "flowers") who certainly accompanied the group and may even refer ironically to P'i's own status as a *pang-hua* (literally, "flower of the examination list or placard"—someone who was passed because of his unusual surname)[98].

The following year Cheng Yü departed to take up the position of Prefect of Canton. Thus, even if P'i had been on good terms with his examiner, this aegis would have been removed at precisely the time when it was vital for his career. As a Southerner, moreover, Cheng Yü seems to have been awarded the position of examiner as a reward for his loyal service. His ties with the court, often essential in attempting to find positions for one's students, could not have been strong. Still following the traditional route to an official career, however, P'i attempted the *Po-hsüeh hung-tz'u* examination, usually deemed a prerequisite for success, in 868.[99] He failed. Both anecdotal evidence and P'i's own writings suggest that this was not the only failure of this first sojourn in Ch'ang-an. P'i's didactic *Literary Marsh* certainly could not have been well received in the profligate milieu that was then the T'ang capital. He seems to have had few friends and established no permanent residence in the city.[100] There is a marked lack of references to capital sights or acquaintances in his writings. Thus disillusioned and still with no position in the capital bureaucracy, he left Ch'ang-an later that year, apparently intending to return to the villa in Shou-chou.[101]

V   *Sojourn in Soochow*

Historians hypothesize that P'i's original destination was Shou-chou and that en route, on learning of P'ang Hsün's revolt, he went to Soochow to circumvent it.[102] P'i himself, however, merely states that he came to Soochow to avoid the rebel troops.[103] It is of interest to note, moreover, that Ling-hu T'ao was reassigned at this time, suggesting that P'i may have started out to join him, and then moved on to Soochow when he was informed of Ling-hu's departure. Whatever the original goal, P'i arrived in Soochow in 869, after what seems to have been a leisurely journey.[104] Later that year a new prefect, Ts'ui P'u, arrived and gave P'i what amounted to a sinecure in his retinue.[105]

During this stay in Soochow, P'i's life was to undergo great changes. Shortly after his arrival, Lu Kuei-meng (d. *ca.* 881) came with some of his writings to pay P'i a visit.[106] Lu was from an aristocratic family which had inhabited the area for centuries. Although he had attempted the *chin-shih* examination once, he was known as a recluse with a huge library and as a connoisseur of tea. Through Lu Kuei-meng P'i was able to meet most of the prominent local intellectuals. He formed a friendship with the recluse, Hsü Hsiu-chü, and often borrowed books from Hsü's large library.[107] The extensive interest in local Soochow history and mythology came, no doubt, from these books, as did the problems P'i encountered with his vision at the time.[108]

It seems that well-known literati of the region, such as Lo Yin, were absent during the years of P'i's sojourn.[109] However, as Lu's courtesy visit demonstrates, P'i had already acquired a literary reputation of his own, based primarily on the *Literary Marsh*.[110] He was acquainted with the Japanese monk, Ensai (*ca.* 800–877), who was at this time waiting to return to Japan. A monk from Silla (modern Korea), moreover, came to Soochow to ask P'i to write an epitaph for a Ch'an master who had recently died.[111] The eulogizing poems that some of the members of the Soochow literary coterie wrote to P'i also demonstrate his literary status.[112] Indeed, during P'i's short residence in Soochow a group of many prominent local poets gathered about him.[113] When the poetic output of the group for the first year was collected by Lu Kuei-meng in his *Sung-ling chi* [Pine Knoll Anthology], it amounted to nearly seven hundred poems, about half composed by P'i. Though these poems mark P'i's last important literary productions, their personal tenor differs greatly from his early didactic work. This development may be the normal result of artists coming to feel a "hopeless contradiction between their aims and the aims of the society to which they belong," as the critic Georgi Plekhanov claims.[114] At any rate, P'i seems to have

reached the stage when he felt frustrated and began to realize that a
political career under the T'ang government was hopeless.[115] This
change may also, however, illustrate Lu Kuei-meng's influence.

His personal life was transformed as well. Since P'i demonstrates
in his verse a fascination with the region's most famous beauty, Hsi
Shih,[116] it is not a great surprise to discover that he married a local
girl at this time.[117] P'i never specifically refers to his wife in his
extant corpus, but she is certainly the partner with whom he shares
his sorrow in the following poem:

Grieving for Our Daughter

Still not even one year old,
Why are the Nine Springs so deep?
All that remains is this "scroll grass";
Facing one another we share the heartache.[118]

The Nine Springs refers, of course, to the Chinese netherworld.
"Scroll grass" is a type of plant which continues to grow even when
its "heart" is plucked out. This tiny piece of the natural world sym-
bolizes P'i's emotional state. The last line is ambiguous, stressing
either the heartache shared by P'i and the grass, or by P'i and
someone else (his wife in this translation).

In 872–873 P'i may have followed Ts'ui P'u when the latter was
transferred (as prefect) to T'ung-chou (modern Ta-li County in
Shensi Province). Returning to Soochow shortly after a new emperor, Hsi-tsung (r. 874–888), took the throne, P'i left for Ch'ang-an
in the late summer of 877.[119] During this year his first son, P'i
Kuang-yeh (877–943), was born.[120] Once in Ch'ang-an he was appointed Adjunct Secretary in Charge of Redaction (Chu-tso tso-
lang)[121] and then Professor at the National University (Kuo-tzu po-
shih). In 878 or 879 another son, Kuang-lin, was born,[122] but very
little other detail is known of P'i's life during this period.

No doubt the classical study P'i claims he engaged in while in
Soochow prepared him for such positions, but whether the ap-
pointments were the result again of his political connections or of his
growing literary renown is impossible to determine. In 880 he was
appointed Deputy Commissioner (Fu-shih) of P'i-ling, a commandery in Ch'ang-chou, and presumably set out at once for the Soochow
area again. En route he encountered Huang Ch'ao and his horde
heading for the capital.[123]

VI *Service with Huang Ch'ao*

Before discussing this last phase of P'i's life, and especially the circumstances leading to his death, the reader must be reminded that the implications of joining a peasant rebellion in traditional China are extremely far-reaching and thus controversial. Conclusions of Marxist scholars, anxious to list P'i as a revolutionary, people's poet, are bound to contradict accounts written by P'i's descendants, whether they were related to him by blood or merely by spirit. However, since this study is primarily concerned with the literary aspects of P'i's life, only a brief account of this enigmatic affair will be provided. Basically, there are three theories concerning P'i's relationship with Huang, all derived from traditional source material: 1) that P'i never met or joined Huang Ch'ao, 2) that he was executed by T'ang loyalists after serving Huang, and 3) that he was put to death by Huang Ch'ao because of a riposte.[124] Quite naturally one would expect the first hypothesis to have been that of P'i's clan members. The second originated from various traditional authors. And the third, also based on traditional texts, has been the raison d'être of much of the interest in P'i by scholars in the People's Republic.

Most evidence indicates, however, that P'i did join Huang Ch'ao in the fall of 880 as Huang swept from Huai-nan west and north to the capital.[125] Such a commitment to a social rebel like Huang is not inconsistent with either P'i's temperament or his politics.[126] It may have seemed to him a chance to put into practice his earlier ideas on politics and government, as found in the *Literary Marsh*. According to the account of the rebel given in the *Chiu T'ang shu* (Old T'ang History), many scholars and officials who had retired during the troubles of the early years of the reign of the boy emperor, Hsi-tsung, now joined Huang Ch'ao.[127]

After arriving in Ch'ang-an early in 881, P'i was made a Han-lin Academician. There are no extant works by P'i from this era and thus one can only speculate concerning his reaction to the new government. The city itself had suffered greatly as the following excerpt from Wei Chuang's (836–910) "Lament of the Lady of Ch'in" illustrates:

> Supporting the infirm and leading children by the hand,
>   fugitives are calling to one another in the turmoil;

Some clamber on to roofs, others scale walls, and all
   is in disorder.
Neighbours in the south run into hiding with neighbours
   in the north,
And those in the east make for shelter with those in
   the west.
Our northern neighbour's womenfolk, trooping all together,
Dash wildly about in the open like stampeding cattle.
Boom, boom!—Heaven and earth shake with the rumbling
   of chariot wheels,
And the thunder of ten thousand horses' hoofs re-echoes
   from the ground.
Fires burst out, sending golden sparks high up into
   the firmament,
And the twelve official thoroughfares are soon seething
   with smoke and flame.[128]

Nevertheless, P'i had shown interest in Liu Pang, the peasant leader who founded the Han dynasty amidst similar chaos.[129] Thus, despite the destruction evident everywhere in the capital city, the unruliness of its populace, and the instability of the central government, P'i no doubt foresaw the possibility of a gradual rebuilding under an enlightened coterie of top advisors.[130] The Han after all had begun sacking Hsien-yang. But the situation in the early 880s was not that of the late third century B.C., and Huang Ch'ao was no Liu Pang. Huang could not accept the criticism and admonitions of the scholars in his retinue. The two and a half years during which his Ta-Ch'i dynasty ruled Ch'ang-an seems to have been in fact a period of terror for the literati.[131] Many of the new regime's officials may have been recruited from the ranks of Huang's armies.

Wei Chuang narrates again:

Their clothes are put on all awry, the language they
   speak is strange;
Overweening pride in their prowess is writ large in
   their faces.
Their officers of the Cypress Terrace are a lot of
   cunning foxes,
Their members of the Orchid Office are so many slinking
   rats.

> In their close-cropped hair they would fain stick orna-
>   mental hairpins,
> Without removing their Court robes they roll themselves
>   in embroidered coverlets.
> Clutching their ivory tablets upside down, they masquerade
>   as Ministers of State;
> With the golden fish at their girdles wrong way up, they
>   play the part of Court official.
> In the morning I hear them entering the Audience
>   Chamber to present their memorials,
> But in the evening one sees them brawling as they make
>   their way to the wine tavern.[132]

To make things even worse, in 882 Huang became enraged over a placard criticizing his government which had been posted on one of the gates to the Department of Affairs of State *(Shang-shu sheng)* and executed many literati, thus further depleting the ranks of ex- perienced bureaucrats.[133] The ambience of the capital must have been particularly volatile for P'i, whose hubris is not belied by any of his biographers. In a poem probably written at about this time (Ogawa Shōichi believes that this verse may have led to P'i's execution), "On the Crab," one senses an admiration for (or even a symbolic identification with) this brazen crustacean:[134]

> Before I'd journeyed to the sea, I already knew his name;
> He has bones, but they grow atop his flesh.
> Don't say being insentient he dreads thunder and lightning!
> He even dares to sidle about in the dragon king's palace![135]

Thus the theory that P'i was killed by Huang Ch'ao for his insolence may merit consideration. According to one anecdote, when P'i was ordered to "analyze" Huang Ch'ao's name, he described Huang's given name as "three crooked lines atop a fruit."[136] Since Huang was ugly and balding, he took offense and had P'i executed. This explanation of P'i's death seems logical. A Han-lin Academician would have been called upon for such matters as "character analysis." Moreover, P'i may have been disillusioned with the lack of social or governmental reform in the years since Huang had taken the capital—amidst the confused battles between Huang's armies and minions of the T'ang court very little actual governing could

have been possible. The city itself, as Wei Chuang paints it, was
further desecrated:

> Fuel-gatherers have hacked down every flowering plant
>   in the Apricot Gardens,
> Builders of barricades have destroyed the willows along
>   the Imperial Canal.
> All the gaily-coloured chariots with their ornamented
>   wheels are scattered and gone,
> Of the stately mansions with their vermilion gates less
>   than half remain.[137]

This wanton havoc caused many to lose faith in Huang's right to
rule. And P'i was not adept at feigning respect. It is known, for
example, that he had almost lost his life by carelessly offending the
Military Governor of Chiang-hsia, Liu Yün-ch'ang.[138] Liu had en-
tertained P'i for some time as a guest, but the latter came intoxicated and quite tardy to a feast given in his honor. Moreover, he
insulted one of Liu's closest retainers. Finally, Liu could stand no
more and asked if he realized that nearby was Parrot Island, where
Huang Tsu (d. 208) had had his notoriously eccentric guest, Ni
Heng (171–196), drowned because of Ni's impudence.[139] It seems,
indeed, that with P'i's obdurate temper and constant vacillation
between reclusive desires and the wish to serve someone worthy,
he had long ago come to consider himself a man in Ni Heng's mold,
as can be seen in his "A Spring Outing in Hsiang-chou:"

> Let the horse have his head as prancing and dancing we go,
> The spring breeze leads us along and inspires poetic
>   feelings.
> Living so easy everything encountered becomes a song;
> Carelessly crashing parties one ought to hide one's name.
> Judging a man midst dazzling willows oft leads to error,
> Peeking at birds through the flowers one can distinguish
>   them best.
> When did I wear a musician's cap, a sheer silk robe?
> Don't say I'm stark-raving mad like Ni Heng.[140]

Although this poem cannot be precisely dated, one senses again that
a patronage (either a particular man or potential patrons in general)
is referred to here. The poem is built around the story of Ni Heng's

reception by the satrap, Ts'ao Ts'ao (155–220).[141] Though Ni had been recommended to the general, he refused to visit him, arguing that Ts'ao should come to him instead. Thus when Ni finally joined Ts'ao's retinue, the latter gave a feast and ordered Ni, who could play the drums, to put on a military drummer's uniform—a cap and a sheer silk robe. But Ts'ao's attempt to humiliate him failed, for Ni avenged himself when he stood up to change into the uniform during the feast and calmly stripped off all his clothes. The third couplet argues that no one can be properly evaluated unless the observer is undetected and the subject in his own natural environs (Ni's home rather than Ts'ao's headquarters). In the final lines, however, one sees P'i's clear personal identification with the overweening Ni Heng. To this self-conception, it would seem, P'i remained loyal until his death in 883.

VII   *Concluding Remarks*

In constructing a biography of P'i Jih-hsiu one is hampered by the paucity of reliable historical data. Yet the anecdotal sources are at least somewhat consistent. Based upon these sources and theories on the types of behavior which might have been produced by the social changes of the ninth century, one might consider P'i's youth to have been distinguished by rituality, as he determined to pursue an official career (accepting the traditional means), despite misgivings about government service (rejecting the traditional goal). Yet there are also innovative aspects of this period, such as his New Music Bureau verse, which was intended to circumvent traditional means of addressing the emperor. After his examination success brought him no recognition, however, he retreated (rejecting both the goals and the means of the scholar-official) to the Soochow literary coteries. Finally, seeing in Huang Ch'ao and his regime both a new set of goals and new procedures for attaining them, P'i became, and died, a rebel. Although these conclusions are necessarily speculative, they do provide a meaningful framework through which P'i's life can be viewed.

CHAPTER 2

Changes of a Literary Mind:
Literary Criticism

I Introduction

IT often seems useful to survey the literary-critical tenets of an author before examining his works. This is certainly so for P'i Jih-hsiu, who attempts to justify or explain his pendulous shifts from didacticism to aestheticism in various prefaces and literary manifestos. In following several previous discussions, most of the critical terminology employed in this chapter will be based upon M. H. Abrams' *The Mirror and the Lamp*[1] and James J. Y. Liu's *The Art of Chinese Poetry*[2] and *Chinese Theories of Literature*.[3] This immediately presents a problem, since much of P'i's early work and a proportionate share of his critical comments are addressed to prose writings, whereas Liu's theories are confined to the norm of Chinese literary theory—lyricism. Nevertheless, Liu's schematization (derived from Abrams) of criticism as consisting of six basic groups, depending on emphases of the relationships between universe—writer—work—reader—universe, and his division of the artistic process into the four phases of universe affecting artist, artist responding with his creation, creation affecting audience, and the resultant change in audience response to the universe, prove useful in treating all of P'i's corpus.[4] Based upon this paradigm Liu proposes that there are six basic theories of literature:

1. Metaphysical. Literature is viewed as a manifestation of the basic universal principle, *tao* (stresses universe—writer link).
2. Deterministic. Considers literature to be the unconscious reflection of the relations between the universe and society (stresses universe—writer).
3. Expressive. Literature is a projection of the author's own feelings into external objects (writer—work).

4. Technical. Literature is judged to be deliberate composition (work—author).
5. Aesthetic. Literature is considered to be beautiful verbal patterns (work—reader).
6. Pragmatic. Literature is seen as the means to effect political and social change (universe—reader).

Having established this distribution, Liu cautions that most Chinese critics are eclectic or syncretic,[5] and that they pay "lip service to [the pragmatic concept] while actually focusing attention on other concepts . . . or simply kept silent about the pragmatic concept while developing others."[6] He points out that this pragmatic concept dominated the T'ang and Sung eras, with the exception of some deviation in the late T'ang and Five Dynasties period.[7]

In looking closer at these late T'ang developments, one might be able to present a case for at least two tendencies: the major and seemingly most influential[8] being the expressive (with overtones of technical-aesthetic), and a contratrend of pragmatism. Previous evaluations of P'i's critical stance have been sharply divided as to his allegiance. Shen Te-ch'ien (1673–1769) in the *T'ang-shih pieh-tsai* [A Supplementary Collection of T'ang Poetry] stresses the expressive-aesthetic orientation of P'i's work (this and subsequent classifications apply James J. Y. Liu's terminology to the various critics' evaluations).[9] Some modern scholars concur: Lo Ken-ts'e follows Shen's assessment in his discussion of P'i's "eremitic theories."[10] Ogawa Shōichi emphasizes P'i's pragmatic tendencies.[11] Most scholars from the People's Republic apologize for his aestheticism, and emphasize that P'i's major contribution was on the pragmatic side.[12] Miao Yüeh, however, suggests P'i was influenced by both schools.[13] In an attempt to resolve this question and to arrive at an independent conclusion, one needs to examine P'i's attitude toward his contemporaries and his own works. Thus, in the discussion below, P'i's evaluations of other T'ang literati will be examined first (his descriptive criticism), before turning to his opinions and theories of his own work (prescriptive ideas).

II *P'i's Descriptive Comments on Other T'ang Writers*

One salient impression of a perusal of P'i's works is that he was quite well read. The classics (with an emphasis on *Mencius*, which was at that time not yet considered a classic), many historical works, the major works of the "major" poets, philosophical collections, anecdotal works, Taoist and Buddhist tomes, as well as numerous contemporary authors are mentioned or alluded to in P'i's writings. This is indeed exactly what one might expect of a man who served as a Professor at the National University. Yet, although P'i's conception of the history of Chinese literature up to his own era was close to that which one finds in modern accounts,[14] his personal preferences in reading were not always guided by this objective overview.

Thus, although P'i mentions Tu Fu several times and seems to have modeled at least one series of poems on Tu's work,[15] he gives us no "reading" or interpretation of Tu's verse. He refers more often to Li Po, but seems to admire him more for his life-style than his verse.[16]

P'i's comments on the *Book of Poetry*, however, illustrate one important aspect of his descriptive criticism. In a morally pedantic essay entitled "Cheng Shen Yüeh 'P'ing-lun *Shih*'" [Correcting Shen Yüeh's (441–513) "Critical Discussion of the *Book of Poetry*"],[17] he attacks both the Mao Commentary and Shen's interpretation of a passage from the *Book of Poetry*. His criticism of the *Han-shih wai-chuan* (Han Ying's Illustrations of the Didactic Application of the Classic of Songs) is quite similar.[18] This scholastic tendency is certainly a carry-over from the critical scholarship on the *Spring and Autumn Annals*.[19]

In treating Meng Hao-jan, who was also from Hsiang-yang, P'i is more specific. In "Ying-chou Meng-t'ing chi" [Record of Meng (Hao-jan)'s Pavilion in Ying-chou], after an introductory section depicting the greatness of the poetry written during Emperor Hsüantsung's reign (713–755), as represented by Li Po and Tu Fu, and an impressionistic evaluation of Meng Hao-jan's talents, P'i examines the relationship between Meng's verse and that of his predecessors: "The Northern Ch'i (550–78) admired Hsiao Chüeh[20] and has [the lines]: 'The hibiscus flowers under dew droop, The willow leaves in the moonlight spread apart.'[21] Meng[Hao-jan] has [the lines]: 'Thin clouds dissipate the Milky Way, Sparse rain drops on the Wu-t'ung tree.'[22] . . . all showing that he was able to slightly overcome the ancients."[23] This passage, aside from illustrating again P'i's catholic knowledge of Chinese poetry[24] (he goes on to compare Meng's verse to precursory lines in Wang Jung [467–493] and Hsieh T'iao [464–499]), suggests that P'i was most conscious of the influence of earlier poets and of the resistance by the T'ang literatus to it[25]—a topic which has elicited considerable interest among contemporary critics.[26] His comments in this piece speak to literature not merely from the point of view of an admirer of Meng Hao-jan's verse, but also as a late T'ang poet seeking "to overcome the ancients" and their influence. It is this concept which raises this short passage, for the twentieth-century reader at least, above the level of most *shih-hua* (poetry-talk) critiques.

The other poet to receive considerable critical attention in his writings is Po Chü-i. Although much of P'i's final poem in his "Poems on the Seven Beloved," "Po T'ai-fu" [Grand Tutor Po], is devoted to the latter's character, it merits citation in toto:

> I love Po Chü-i,
> Extraordinary talent born of spontaneity.
> Who could call him a utensil of verbiage and pen?
> He's rather a sage who discourses on the classics.
> 5 Suddenly from a poem of superficial beauty,
> He shapes a piece like a canon or announcement.[27]
> In his actions the one hundred (virtuous) behaviors are
>   fulfilled,
> In his writings the six modes[28] are completed.
> A pure model outstanding among the court,
> 10 With upright tones he shook the censorate's walls.
> What he offered as criticism was well thought out,
> What he imitated must have been worthy of transmission.
> Forgetting his body, he gave himself to poetry and wine,
> Giving reign to his lofty ideas, he was partial to mountain
>   and glade.
> 15 He had hoped to top the literary scene;
> He wished to hold the power of producing reform.
> How could he expect that he would have encountered slander?
> By holding to the middle road he was often sent to the
>   left [i.e., demoted].
> When all under heaven were striving hard,
> 20 Lo-t'ien [i.e., Po] alone was content [not to strive].[29]
> When all under heaven were troubled,
> Lo-t'ien was the only one to "put it aside."[30]
> Chanting loudly, he declined the two side-apartments,[31]
> Whistling clearly, he withdrew from the three rivers.[32]
> 25 As a retired scholar he resembled a lone crane,
> He abandoned honors as a cicada sheds skins.
> In service he didn't obtain his heart's desire,
> But he could serve as turtle or mirror for it.[33]

P'i's concerns in this piece are with the four phases of the artistic process as characterized by James J. Y. Liu: 1) universe affecting writer; 2) writer's response producing work; 3) work reaching and affecting reader; and 4) modification of reader's response to universe. The spontaneity (line 2 in the poem) and yet the dependence on the classics (line 4), the six modes (line 8), and the poem of superficial beauty (line 5) illustrate that the universe of Po Chü-i (or any Chinese poet) includes both natural and literary spheres. Although inspiration may come from a striking landscape, it is most often filtered through a mind filled with previous descriptions and literary formulas of landscapes in general. In responding to such stimuli, Po has been able to transcend the tendency of the poetaster, a mere "utensil of verbiage and pen" (line 3) to produce works of classic quality (which thus are worthy to serve as models themselves). The effect and the modification of this response to the universe can be seen in line 10: "With upright tones he shook the censorate's walls." Indeed, P'i equates great literature with social efficacy in lines 15–16. The rest of the poem deals with a fifth phase (although one might actually see it as a repeated phase one), wherein the poet, Po Chü-i, reacts to the reader's response (or lack of it) to withdraw from society and serve as the model sage. This interpretation certainly bespeaks P'i's own personal predilections as much as biographical fact.

P'i again addresses the question of the poet's reaction to the universe in another piece on Po Chü-i, "Lun Po Chü-i chien Hsü Ning ch'ü Chang Hu" (On Po Chü-i's Recommending Hsü Ning and Disparaging Chang Hu): "I have stated that the difficulty in composition is the difficulty in one's source of inspiration. Yüan [Chen] and Po [Chü-i]'s hearts were rooted in establishing the proper teachings, and thus they allegorized in the harmonious and obliging diction of Music Bureau verses, saying that they were satirical or were expressing their own feelings.[34] After they advocated this and achieved a great reputation, contemporary scholars have all united to follow them, imitating their diction, but losing their intent."[35]

Here it is clearly stated that the author's response to the universe is of paramount importance. Yüan Chen and Po Chü-i, in P'i's estimation, were the only then modern poets who had responded properly. P'i's own contemporaries had not understood that the "Yüan-Po style" had little to do with the diction or the genre of the New Music Bureau poems, but was based entirely on motivation or intent. Even in P'i's later tendency toward technical and expressive poetry, he maintained his adherence to this tenet, by avoiding any pretense to social consciousness.

But most of his theoretical literary concepts are presented in the prefaces P'i wrote to the two major collections of his verse, and they are the subject of the next section.

III   *P'i's Prescriptive Criticism: Prefaces to His Own Works*

To find P'i Jih-hsiu's prescriptive theories of literature one must turn to the prefaces he wrote for his *Literary Marsh*, for Lu Kuei-meng's *Pine Knoll Anthology*, and for several of his individual works. Since these collections are quite dissimilar and depict a change in P'i's critical concepts, they shall be examined chronologically.

"Preface to the *Literary Marsh of Master P'i*"

In the *ping-hsü* year of the Hsien-t'ung reign period [866] P'i Jih-hsiu took the examinations, did not pass, and retired to a villa east of the prefectural seat of Shou to edit his writings, intending to present them then to someone in office. When he opened his file box, there was a thicket [of writings] as abundant as if in a marsh; therefore, he named this book *Literary Marsh*. Recently he saw that Yüan Chieh had presented his literary works to an official, the Vice-President (of the Ministry of Rites), Mr. Yang Chün, who, when he saw the works, sighed and said, "To pass Master Yüan in the examinations, even at the top, would be to sully him."[36] These writings cannot presume to call forth Mr. Yang's sighs, but only to become known among contemporary writers.

The prose-poem belongs to the modes of ancient poetry.[37] When P'i was distressed that the previous kings had been indulgent, he wrote the "Prose-poem on Concern." When he was anxious about keeping up the road the people have to tread, he wrote the "Prose-poem on the River Bridge." Mindful that the feelings of the people did not have access to the emperor, he wrote the "Prose-poem on Mount Huo." And when he felt empathy for the obscurity of poor scholars, he wrote the "Prose-poem on the Peach Blossom."

Because the "Encountering Sorrow," the flower of all literature, suffers from profundity and abstruseness and one is not able to elucidate it today, he wrote the "Nine Satires." Literature prizes tracing intrinsic principles, and intrinsic principles prize the original state of things. Thus he wrote the "Ten Origins." Since the Grand Musicians died out and the Perfect Tones have not been transmitted, he wrote the "Nine Great Songs" to supplement the *Rites of Chou* (Chou-li). During the two Han dynasties rather middling scholars held our Mr. Tso [Tso Ch'iu-ming] lightly, and thus he wrote the

"[Ten Essays] Resolving Doubtful Passages in the *Spring and Autumn Annals.*"

As for the rest—tablet inscriptions, epitaphs, eulogies, tributes, disquisitions, expositions, letters, and prefaces—they are all either designed to refute distant wrongs of antiquity, or to remedy recent omissions of modern times and are not just empty words. When the doctrine *(tao)* [in these writings] is compared [to the classics or to the above mentioned writings such as the "Encountering Sorrow" which served as P'i's model], it is seen to be definitely inferior to that of the ancients.

He has brought together old-style poems at the end of this collection, so that in looking through them one may obtain a somewhat delicious taste in the mouth, just as when eating fish one may chance upon a delicacy, or in taking meat one may discover a specially tender piece. The "Genealogical Record of Master P'i," which he placed at the end, has the same significance as the Great Historian's (Ssu-ma Ch'ien) autobiographical postface. In all there are two hundred pieces forming ten *chüan*—may you readers not be led to ridicule.[38]

As a modern statement of literary theory, P'i's "*Marsh* Preface" would merit little interest, yet although he does not present a theory of literature, he does attend to the question of the relationship of the author to the literary tradition and to his social environment according to the following pattern: 1) the writer senses some social injustice, 2) he selects the proper genre or work as model, and 3) he composes a contemporary piece in the tradition of his model. This tripartite system is standard enough, but P'i, again in the style of the radical classical scholarship of the T'ang, points to where it has ceased to function: the obsolescence of the "Encountering Sorrow," he claims, renders the work ineffectual; the ancient *ya* (classical) music has been lost, damaging the possibilities for the moral suasion of Music Bureau pieces; and finally, the disarray of the commentaries to the *Spring and Autumn Annals* undermines the importance of this classic.

The concept of an author inferable from this preface, moreover, is similar to that of Ts'ao P'i's (187–226) "universal talent," *t'ung-ts'ai*, a master of all "proper genres." Although a polygraph, his primary role is to make known the problems in the empire and, through commentary or supplementation of the classics, to suggest some means to solve them. One further senses that an author is the man who has been entrusted with keeping literature (i.e., The Classics) current, with revising or rewriting its exegesis, and with pointing out the most appropriate significance of a particular work for the present day. Criticism itself is never openly the subject of this preface. Yet P'i clearly implies that the determination, the definition, and the proper exegesis of the classical corpus, so that it will be eternally capable of influencing the people, is its primary function.

P'i's comment (based upon an allusion to the "Hsi-tz'u" section of the *I ching*[39]) that "literature prizes tracing intrinsic principles" foreshadows the scientific *ko-wu* (investigation of things) spirit associated with Neo-Confucian thought. Other Confucian influences may be seen in other allusions to canonical works,[40] as well as in the doctrinal succession implied in the precedent case of Yüan Chieh (719–772), the indirect allusion to Han Yü (in using the genre of "origins" [*yüan*] which Han made famous), and in the proto-Confucian T'ang exegetical concern with the *Spring and Autumn Annals*.

But perhaps the most prominent concept in this preface is that of formal literature *(wen)* as 1) consisting almost entirely of the classics and their exegesis, and 2) functioning as a didactic tool. Even the prose-poem, which during certain periods in Chinese literary history marked the apotheosis of euphuistic writings, is theoretically restored herein to its earlier admonitory function. This typically *ku-wen* (neoclassical) stance is in some ways a reaction to the major anthology available to the T'ang reader, the *Wen hsüan*. Genres derived from the *Wen hsüan*, in fact, such as tablet inscriptions, epitaphs, and expositions, are apologetically appended with P'i's poetry in the final chapter of the *Literary Marsh*. And P'i feels the necessity to assure the reader that they "are not just empty words."

Yet despite the orthodox attitude toward author, literature, critic, and criticism presented in this preface, one notices a latent prizing of poetry in P'i's metaphoric comments that "one may chance upon a delicacy" therein.

Ten of these "delicacies" can be found in the series "Cheng Yüeh-fu" [Orthodox Music Bureau Ballads], perhaps P'i's best known works. These ballads, too, were inspired by Yüan Chieh. Yüan's "Hsi yüeh-fu shih-erh shou" [Twelve Verses Propagating the Music Bureau Ballad], however, were intended to carry on the traditional, critical function of the *yüeh-fu*.[41] Under Po Chü-i and Yüan Chen the so-called "New Music Bureau Ballads" *(hsin yüeh-fu)* shaped Yüan Chieh's experiments into a genre of sorts. Subsequent poets had, however, turned this form back to Six Dynasties influences (see the excerpt from "On Po Chü-i's Recommending Hsü Ning and Disparaging Chang Hu" above), and thus P'i felt the need to again return the genre to orthodoxy. His preface states:

Music Bureau ballads are those songs collected by the sage kings of antiquity, desiring through them to understand the strengths and weaknesses of the country, the joys and sorrows of the people. . . . The beauty of these songs was sufficient to exhort listeners to meritorious efforts. The moral force of these songs was enough to admonish rulers with regard to governing. Therefore, the duty of the Grand Master according to the *Rites of Chou* was to direct the teaching of the six (modes of) poetry, and the duty of the Lesser Master to direct the chanting of poetry. In light of this, the way of the Music Bureau ballad is great! The so-called Music Bureau ballads today, however, are merely the lavish extravagance of the Wei and Tsin periods, the ethereal beauty of the Ch'en and Liang eras. To call them Music Bureau songs is really not at all correct![42]

These didactic ideas, stressing the third and fourth phases of the artistic process, are echoed in several works in the *Literary Marsh*, but are perhaps best tied together with P'i's comments on the function of literature in his essay "On the Origin of Moral Influence": "Heaven is not able to repress disorder, for it does not produce a sage generation after generation. Yet its Way *(tao)* is preserved in words, and its teachings persist in literature."[43] In other words, literature is heaven's record on earth, the substitute sage to direct peaceful rule in the interim between the appearances of the sages themselves. Such a theory, it should be noted, is eminently befitting a young examination candidate and its espousal certainly could not have failed to aid P'i's success in the examinations of 867.

Scarcely a half-dozen years later P'i's position, his environment, and his literary views, as found in the "Preface to the *Pine Knoll Anthology*," had been greatly altered:

Poetry has six modes, one of which is called analogy *(pi)*. Analogy, the determination of the inner feelings and outer form of things, must be called a talent. This talent at its fullest with regard to sages is embodied in the six classics and with regard to the virtuous lies in music. Unfortunately, after the period of Spring and Autumn the paeans [*sung*] were lost. When we come to the House of Han the doctrines of poetry were continued, but the custom of the *ya*-odes had been abandoned and could not be revived.

With reference to poetry there are compositions of three words (per line), of four words, of five words, of six and of seven. An example of the three-word type would be: "There throng (the) egrets,/ Egrets in flight."[44] An example of the five-word would be: "Who says (the) sparrow (has) no beak?/ How else (could it) peck (through) my house?"[45] The six-word: "Meanwhile I pour (out a cup from) that bronze *lei*-vase."[46] The seven-word: "Crosswise fly (the) yellow birds, (they) settle on (the) mulberry (trees)."[47] An example of the nine-word would be: "Far (away we) draw (water from) that running pool; (we) ladle (it) there (and) pour (it out) here."[48] In old-style poetry the four-word (line) was basic, but from the House of Han on it was written in five- and seven-word (lines). These verses also emerged from Chou dynasty poetry. Li Ling's "Holding hands, ascending the river bridge,"[49] is an example of a five-word line. As for seven-word lines, there is Emperor Wu (of Han)'s "The sun, moon and heavenly bodies (stars and planets) are in harmony with the four seasons."[50] Thereafter (these forms) flourished during the Chien-an era (196–220) and the following periods. Those rulers and statesmen who lived "on the left bank of the River,"[51] attained to a volatile beauty, but the six modes of poetry were obscured. When we reach the K'ai-yüan generation (713–742) of our T'ang dynasty, poets changed their form to "regulated," and started to press lines into elegant parallelism, constrained by tonal features. In the *Book of Poetry* one reads: "The distresses I met with are many,/ I received insults not a few."[52] This parallelism is skillfully done. In the "Canon of Yao" one reads: ". . . Notes accompany the chanting, and pitch-pipes harmonize the notes."[53] This sort of regulation is extreme!

From Han to T'ang the concepts of poetry have consisted in no more than this. Moreover, I can't foresee what the concept of poetry will be like a thousand years hereafter, or whether it will simply stop here. If there are to be later changes in composition, I am not able to know of them.

When talent is fulfilled, isn't it rather like the vital force *(ch'i)* of heaven and earth?[54] The vital force rests in its unity. When it is divided into the four seasons, it takes the form of spring and

> shines upon withered branches and
>   brings forth sprouts,
> whether nurturing or protecting,
> it blends with all nature
> and intoxicates mankind in flesh and bone.

It takes the form of summer and

> is the bright light of dawn
>   ascending,   ·
> when heaven and earth like a kiln

scorch grasses and bake trees,
and seem to singe man's coat of
    bodily hair.

Of autumn and

the breezes of Boreas, high trans-
    parent skies
which seem to reveal the framework
    of Heaven;
crisp panoramas and evenings clear,
spirit not concealing form.

Its wintry nature

as a sheet of frost descends in
    bitter cold,
all creation withers together,
clouds occlude and the sun pales,
as if in fear of Heaven's reprimand

If this is so, how can it [the vital force] be confined to a single form? The answer is it simply transforms. If those who have talent don't transform it, it is all right. But if one transforms it, it is no different than this [i.e., seasonal variations in the vital force]. Therefore, in the application of talent, it can be extensive as the shores of the vast oceans, narrow enough to fit in a drainage ditch, as high as the peaks of mountains, as fragmentary as potsherds, as beautiful as Hsi-tzu, as ugly as Tun Ch'ia, as doughty as the Hu-pen, as languid as a young girl.[55] When it is large, continents cannot hold it, and it cannot be totally explored; when small, then it is the tip of a hair and cannot be seen. If one's talent is such, and one is, moreover, able to use it skillfully, then Cook Ting and his ox, Wheelwright Pien and his wheels, or the axes of Ying wouldn't be enough to be termed "spiritual understandings."[56]

Alas, the gentlemen of antiquity, whether in dire straits or prosperity, found it necessary to express themselves in song. If they desired to show their intent, how could they have done so without literature? Thereupon they wrote their literary compositions. Literary composition is not a skill one can excel in alone—one must have a partner to give it fulfillment. In ancient times when the Duke of Chou wrote a poem, he wrote it to leave for King Ch'eng.[57] And Yin Chi-fu composed a paean to harmonize with a poem of the Earl of Shen.[58] So one knows that presenting poetry has a long history! And subsequent generations have often done this when they wrote poems.

During the seventh year of the Hsien-t'ung reign period (866), when the

present Auxiliary Secretary of the Ministry of War, Ling-hu T'ao, was in
Huai-nan and the present Director of the Decrees in the Imperial Sec-
retariat, the gentleman from Hung-nung, was prefect of P'i-ling,[59] P'i Jih-
hsiu found favor with both through his writings. He was ordered to compose
verse in harmony with their works, enough to fill several books. It also
happened that they asked him to give titles to these collections.[60] During
the tenth year (869) a gentleman of Ch'ing-ho, who was a Censor [Ts'ui P'u],
was sent out as prefect to Wu. P'i became this gentleman's staff secretary.
When he had occupied this post for no more than a month, the *chin-shih* Lu
Kuei-meng,[61] whose style is Lu-wang, took his writings, which were in
several collections, to visit him. His transformation of talent is truly that of
the vital force of heaven and earth. The present era commends Wen
Fei-ch'ing [Wen T'ing-yün] and Li I-shan [Li Shang-yin] as the greatest;
when one compares them to Lu, it is difficult to state who should take
precedence . . . !"[62]

Although this preface is obviously largely intended to praise Lu
Kuei-meng's verse, it is representative of the style of P'i's works
found in this anthology and in his later years in general. Most apparent is the transfer of the critical interest from classical literature to
poetry. This reflects P'i's extant corpus which contains only seven
prose pieces composed after the compilation of the *Literary Marsh*.
Moreover, one finds here a diachronic sense of development which
is missing from P'i's earlier, more universal and theoretical explica-
tions of classical literature.

The poet in this preface is no longer depicted as a multifaceted
talent, but rather as a master of the six modes: analogical, allusive,
descriptive, persuasive, liturgical, and paeanic *(pi, hsing, fu, feng,
ya,* and *sung)*. The attention is no longer on a wide sweep of genres,
but on techniques which could be applied broadly. The poet is
aware of his literary heritage, and not merely an imitator of it. His
task is to know the prosodic possibilities and to allow his innate
talent to transform itself, as the mercurial vital force, *ch'i,* into every
possible manifestation. This emphasis on talent, albeit the talent of a
sort of craftsman, was hardly a concern in P'i's earlier works. The
shift from emphasis on the relationship between the work and the
audience of the earlier didacticism to technical theories which ac-
centuate the ties between the work and the author herein marks a
transformation in P'i's critical thought.

The major critical significance of this preface lies in its rejection of
classical theorists for those of the post-Han period. A great portion

of the text is taken verbatim from Chih Yü's (d. 311) *Wen-chang liu-pieh lun* [Discourse on the Various Schools of Literary Composition].[63] Several other concepts which seem to derive from Ts'ao P'i are apparent, including the importance allotted *ch'i*, the musical analogy, and the idea that literary talent is inherent.[64] The concept of innate literary ability, moreover, can reduce criticism to mere description, historical classification, evaluation, and, at one extreme, to counting the words per line, as we see P'i doing in this preface.

This technical tone is found in most of the works included in this anthology and especially in P'i's "Preface to the *Poetry in Miscellaneous Forms*":

It is on record in the "Canon of Shun" that the Emperor said, "Kuei, I appoint you to be Director of Music and to teach our sons. . . . Poetry expresses earnest thought, singing prolongs the utterance of that expression."[65] And in the *Rites of Chou* it is said: "The duties of the Grand Master are to undertake the teaching of the six poetic (modes)."[66] When the suasive prose-poem flourished, moral influence and elegance were combined in composition, and the various forms took their birth therein. This position was continued in the Music Bureau, probably by the Master of Classical Music. During the Han, Li Yen-nien put the scale in order and thereby created the New Sounds.[67] Although the way of the *ya* was broken off, the Music Bureau verse thus came into splendor. Bell songs and drums and pipes, the duster dances and the *yü* music and its antiphon arose because of this.[68] The form of the lyric cannot but therefore change according to the times. In ancient times the "Musical Treatises" discoursed on this in great detail. Today we do not have the texts in their entirety and have recorded them only from other appearances [i.e., reconstructed them from other texts which quoted excerpts][69]. . . . Alas, from ancient to regulated (style), from regulated to miscellaneous, the way of poetry is thus exhausted therein![70]

Beginning with the "Canon of Shun" maxims, which, as James J. Y. Liu has pointed out, are flexible enough to fit theories of great variety, P'i continues with the idea of transformation he began in the *Pine Knoll* preface. Here, however, it is music accompanying the lyrics which affects their transformation. The didactic content, which P'i stresses in several works cited above, is here forgotten.

IV   *Conclusion*

Attempts to state that P'i Jih-hsiu's literary criticism exhibits any particular trait are certain to prove invalid, for P'i's criticism is a coat of many colors. It changed greatly, moreover, during the 860s and 870s. To try to isolate and define key terms, therefore, is a difficult matter. It is best to deal with his criticism as it appears in a particular work, time period, or critical tendency; but one must be careful not to claim consistency found in these restricted contexts as the critical ideas of P'i Jih-hsiu. One could, perhaps, fix the labels "pragmatic" and "technical" upon the two distinct eras of P'i's criticism.

But as either a pragmatic or a technical critic P'i cannot stand against better known names. His uniqueness lies in his ability to accept his didactic and technical phases without feeling pressured, as so many Chinese critics did, to resolve the two. It is true that as an ideal P'i may have envisioned a classically didactic import presented in the most effective aesthetic form, but the works in his own collections generally adhered either to pragmatic or to technical-aesthetic aspects. It is as a practicing critic, therefore, and a diverse one at that, that P'i deserves attention. He once wrote that "literature has an effect on man which can be compared to that of medicine. When it is skillfully taken, there is a beneficial effect. When it is not so taken, it can on the contrary prove harmful."[71] As can be seen above, literature was a sort of medicine for him. His doses as a young examination candidate were therefore more bitter than those of a decade later, when, surrounded by friends, patrons, disciples, and the heady literary atmosphere of the Soochow region, he naturally felt secure enough to dabble in more exotic drugs.

CHAPTER 3

A Prologue to Neo-Confucianism: Prose

I *Introduction*

THE following pages are concerned primarily with P'i's prose writings. Yet since much of P'i's formal philosophy is expressed in his prose corpus, this chapter will also serve as an overview of his thought. To have entitled it "Philosophy," however, might have been unfair to the reader, since P'i's aesthetics have already been examined in the preceding chapter and since of the remaining four fields of philosophic endeavor—ethics, metaphysics, epistemology, and logic—one finds that P'i, like many Chinese philosophers and most Confucians, is concerned primarily with ethics. That is to say, he is interested in qualities of goodness, in moral duty, in ritual, and in trustworthiness. Moreover, in the history of Chinese thought a line may be drawn between philosophers who consider the order of the universe (cosmology), the nature of being (ontology), etc., and those thinkers who concern themselves primarily with pragmatic matters. At times this division is a tenuous one, but during the chaotic mid-ninth century, or any unsettled era, the rift between these two groups seems to grow. P'i clearly belongs to the latter group.

Other characteristics which should be noted in preparation for reading P'i's prose are his tendency to link moral and political philosophy, his very early appreciation of works such as the *Doctrine of the Mean* (Chung-yung), *Great Learning* (Ta-hsüeh), and *Mencius*, which later become the central corpus of Neo-Confucianism, his attention to classical scholarship, and his reverence of the past as a utopia. By the mid-ninth century, however, this utopia no longer represented a model designed to allow a preservation of the status quo, but had paradoxically become the Golden Past upon which demands for social and political change could be made.

II *Prose Writings*

One sees this clearly in P'i's "Writings of a Recluse at Deer-Gate." This collection of nearly sixty sections was written while P'i was in retirement at Deer-Gate Mountain and was included in his *Literary Marsh*.[1] The format is modeled on earlier analects, such as those of Confucius and Yang Hsiung, and contains several types of aphorisms and brief comments. Often P'i cites some habit or tradition of the past and then shows it to be superior to its contemporary counterpart:

In ancient times the officials considered everything in the empire as their responsibility; therefore, they worried about such things. The officials today consider everything in the empire to be responsible to them; therefore, the people worry about such things (section 12).

Those who withdrew from society in ancient times did so of their own free will; those who withdraw from society today do so in order to gain some advancement in rank through it (section 26).

In ancient times those who sentenced someone to prison and thereby won the people's favor, felt sorrow; those who sentence someone to prison today and thereby win the people's favor, feel joy. Those who felt sorrow were sorry that their moral influence was not effective; those who take joy are happy because they know their bribes will arrive (section 38).

Those who killed men in ancient times did so in a rage; those who kill men today do so with a smile (section 55).

In ancient times a worthy man was employed for the benefit of the state; now he is employed for the benefit of a single family (section 56).

In ancient times drunken rages were caused by wine; today they are caused by the state of mankind (section 57).

In ancient times officials were appointed with the view that they would drive off bandits; today they are appointed with the view that they may become bandits (section 58).

The formulaic structure of "in ancient times . . . , today . . ." is common in both *Mencius* and the *Analects*.[2]

Other passages take the form of short philosophic dissertations:

When the nature of the common people was too violent, the sage guided them with his humanity. When the nature of the common people was too rebellious, the sage guided them with his moral right. When the nature of the common people was too indulgent, the sage guided them with his ritual. When the nature of the common people was too ignorant, the sage guided them with his wisdom. When the nature of the common people was too false, the sage guided them with his trustworthiness. In this way, the sage guided them throughout the empire, the virtuous man guided them in the principalities, and the common man guided them in his home. Those who came thereafter turned guidance into taking, taking into usurpation. Therefore, those who took the empire through humanity were no longer humane once they had it. Those who took a principality through moral right were no longer morally righteous once they had it. Those who took reputation and position through ritual no longer were ritualistic once they had it. Those who took power and influence through wisdom were no longer wise once they had it. Those who took friendship through trust were no longer trustworthy once they had them. Yao and Shun acquired through guidance. They did not take. And having acquired, they were humane. The Yin and Chou dynasties acquired by taking, but having acquired they were still humane. I maintain that since Wang Mang and Ts'ao Ts'ao, those who have practiced humanity, moral right, ritual, wisdom, and trustworthiness were all those who acquired things through usurpation. How sad! (section 2).

What a rudder is to a boat, the Way is to man. If a rudder is unstable, a boat will not behave so that it can go forward without being ruddered. This would be forcing stability out of instability.[3] Human behavior is like that of the boat and its rudder; unless man has the Way, he cannot behave properly, this would be forcing proper behavior where none is possible. Ch'in's losing the rudder to Hsiang Yü, and Hsiang leaving it to the Han dynasty, was the Way of the Sages, in making unstable that which was stabilized. The Way of the petty man is in making stable that which was not (section 16).

P'i's predilection for *Mencius* is particularly evident in section two with its concern for the four cardinal Mencian virtues, humanity *(jen)*, moral right *(i)*, ritual *(li)*, and wisdom *(chih)*, its attention to acquiring the control of the state through guidance, and the setting up of Yao and Shun as examples.[4] The disparaging commentary on Wang Mang (r. 9–23) and Ts'ao Ts'ao would tend to discredit claims by critics in the People's Republic that P'i's thought reveals Legalist influence. The extended metaphor and dense logic of section 16 is common to P'i's style of argumentation.

Finally, there are ethical and moral statements concerning man and his behavior:

Those who slander men, slander themselves. Those who flatter men, flatter themselves. For slanderers are also slandered by others—can't this be said to be slandering oneself? And flatterers are also flattered by others—can't this be said to be flattering oneself? (section 5).

To be able to frighten people and not to do so, to be able to kill and not to do so—this is difficult! (section 10).

To study and then to neglect something is not as good as not studying it and neglecting it. He who has studied something and then neglected it presumes upon his study and is arrogant; arrogance inevitably leads to rudeness. Those who have neglected something without having studied it are ashamed of themselves and humble; humility leads then to perfection (section 22).

When courage exceeds humaneness, one becomes fierce; when talent overwhelms moral force, one becomes rash (section 23).

A little goodness throws moral force into chaos; a little talent can destroy the Way (section 24).

To have a skill and not to bring it forward, to have a talent and not to cultivate it, would be a disgrace for a disciple of Confucius (section 25).

A sage can give man the Way, but he cannot give him the ambition [to follow it] (section 28).

To construct one's ideas without thinking, to set up a friendship without knowledge (of the other person), this is what I fear! (section 34).

Those who slander men lose their uprightness; those who flatter men lose their sincerity; aren't they close to those "honest villagers" (section 43).

Someone said, "I love to build gardens and parks, I love to watch birds and beasts, I love to lead troops, I love to collect taxes." In ancient times people were said to be seditious; now ministers are so depicted (section 45).

Someone asked, "Is it possible to follow the Way of the gentleman regularly?" I replied, "If one does away with the Four Obscurities, and puts the Four Corrections into effect, one can practice it regularly." "What do you mean?" "Seeing virtue and not being able to get close to it, hearing what is moral and not yielding to it, being in the presence of disorder and not putting it straight, or in the presence of profit and not restraining oneself—these are called the Four Obscurities. Not speaking of the Way when it isn't correct, not practicing ritual when it isn't correct, not cultivating literary skills when literature isn't correct, and not calling on a man when he isn't correct—these are known as the Four Corrections" (section 47).

Section 22 recalls the first chapter of the *Analects*: "To learn and at times repeat what one has learnt, is that not after all a pleasure?"[5] And "Master Tseng said, 'Every day I examine myself on these three points: . . . Have I failed to repeat the precepts that have been handed down to me?' "[6] Section 23 is also modeled on the *Analects*: "The Master said, 'Courtesy not bounded by the prescriptions of ritual becomes tiresome. Caution not bounded by the prescriptions of ritual becomes timidity, daring becomes turbulence, inflexibility becomes harshness' ";[7] and "Love of courage without love of learning degenerates into turbulence."[8] Section 28 resembles the *Analects* (see especially Arthur Waley's comment).[9] The *Book of Changes*[10] and the *Analects*[11] are invoked by section 34. The "honest villagers" of section 43 call forth the *Analects* again: "The Master said, 'The "honest villager" spoils true virtue.' "[12] The passage is further explicated in *Mencius*.[13] Section 45 is also related to *Mencius*: "But when those above ignore the rites, those below ignore learning, and seditious people arise, then the end of the state is at hand."[14]

The major concerns of this collection can thus be seen to be those of P'i's social class, of his era, and of P'i himself. The corruption of the government and its decline since the Golden Age of antiquity, an antiquity meant to serve as a model for contemporary reform, is virtually a leitmotiv. Secondary topics include the tribulations of men on the rise in late-ninth-century society (sections 22 and 24 on study, 5 and 43 on slander), the political disintegration of the empire (45 and 56 on the growing strength of the powerful families. 58 on bandits), means of guiding the common people (through literature in section 3 and under a sage in section 2), the question of withdrawal from society (P'i seems to have learned while in retirement that participation was necessary, see sections 25 and 26), and personal ethical models (section 47).

The influence of the more metaphysical Neo-Confucian works such as the *Doctrine of the Mean* and the *Great Learning* can be seen in P'i's study "On the Origin of the Self":

Being able to seek the Way through one's heart—isn't that what we call the self? Being able to perform the duties of the emperor, of the feudal lords, and of the sages with one's heart—isn't that what we call the self? Therefore, the self is not only more important than man, but also more important than the Way. As I have argued before: "One who is capable of insulting the self must be capable of insulting others, one who is capable of slighting the self must be able to slight others, and one who is able to torture the self must be able to torture others. Confucius and Yen Hui were but people who treasured the self. Robber Chih was one who spoiled the self. Therefore, among those scholars of antiquity, there were those who didn't go out of their front door, but whose names carried more weight than Mount Sung or Mount Heng, whose Way was broader than the vast expanse of the ocean; it is all because they respected themselves."

Someone said, "Doesn't the so-called 'reverence of the self' mean not to harm oneself? When Shu Tiao castrated himself, was he fulfilling reverence to the self? Or when Pao Chuang-tzu had his feet cut off, was he fulfilling reverence to the self?"

I replied, "Each both paid reverence and did harm to the self. It is in that one was a flatterer and the other an upright man that they differ. That which is called 'reverence to the self' should be taken to mean doing so according to the Way. Harming the self is also in accordance with the Way."

"A sage toils unwearyingly for the people, to the point that he, like Yao and Shun, tortures himself so that he is like meat cured in the sun and wind.[15] Their labors were indeed extreme, but were they at peace with themselves over this?" he asked.

"Those who labor," I replied, "with their minds, in the labor of a single mind bring peace to the empire. Those like Yü lost all their hair from their thighs and their shinbones, too.[16] His labors were indeed extreme. He who toils with his body, in the toil of a single body can bring peace to a myriad of generations."

"Among the ancients there were those who killed themselves to preserve the principle of humaneness;[17] not a few labored so! What a pity! What I see in today's generation are pleasing smiles and fawning faces, insulting and degrading themselves in undaunted pursuit of success, in a way almost like Shu Tiao."[18]

This piece may have been inspired by Buddhist concern with the same topic. But here, although there may be an implied criticism of Buddhism in the reference to the self-mutilation of Shu Tiao, the emphasis is upon cultivation and protection of the self. P'i first argues metaphorically that Confucius and Yen Hui won fame by respecting themselves. He then turns, guided by the pointed queries of his adversary, to the question of when one can cause oneself harm. Shu Tiao's lord, Duke Huan of Ch'i, was fond of women and very jealous. To gain his favor, Shu castrated himself.[19] Such behavior constituted for P'i flattery of abhorrent type. Pao Chuang-tzu, on the other hand, who reported an adulterous affair, was slandered, and as punishment had his feet cut off,[20] is praised highly. Thus P'i's strong feelings concerning flattery and slander are evident once again. Finally, P'i extols the Mencian idea of self-sacrifice on behalf of peace through the exempla of Yao, Shun, and Yü.[21] The altruism of such efforts is contrasted then with the selfishness of Shu Tiao and P'i's contemporaries.

In an analogic comparison of the human body to the empire, P'i probes the human mind *(hsin)* further:

Preface to the "Six Admonitions"

Master P'i has said that the mind is one's own emperor, the ears and the eyes are the chief ministers, and the four limbs one's feudal lords. If one's emperor is not virtuous, the chief ministers revolt and the feudal lords are thrown into disorder. A good many of those men of antiquity who lost the empire or were bereft of land and home did so because of this. If the single body of the emperor is not virtuous, how can he serve as emperor to all under heaven? Or as master of a land or home? Therefore, I have composed admonitions for the mind, mouth, ears, eyes, hands, and feet, and written them on my girdle. To be at peace and yet not forget danger, to be cautious and not forget moral principles, to be in poverty and not forget integrity, to be of high rank and not forget the Way, and to act as the ancients did, as if one were fitting the two halves of a tally together, doesn't this all lie in the putting into practice of the six admonitions?

Admonition to the Mind

What is conceived as the essence of the great transformation is called man. The spirit of great purity takes form in what is called the mind. The mind is thus the lord, the body the subject.

If inside there is disagreement, the outside will be confused and twisted. The ear grows weary of hearing of morality, and the eyes dislike viewing humanity; the hand holds the handle to disorder, and the foot treads on the doorsill [which is unlucky]. When Shun became emperor, he did not receive veneration. In the case of Shun not commanding respect, the mind was the subject. When Chou Hsin became emperor, he received veneration. In the case of Chou Hsin's receiving veneration, the mind was the lord.

If aside from the emperor, there is no one who commands respect, this is the mind of Chou controlling Chou's body. If aside from the emperor, there is someone who commands respect, this is the mind of Shun controlling Shun's body. (In this situation) how dangerous and alarming for a subject to admonish his lord. The chief ministers (i.e., the eyes and the ears) are not clear, the feudal lords (four limbs) are not obedient. When the lord becomes thus filled with dirt, the subject becomes a common thief.

If one has not reached this (state), it would be best to be diligent (in continuing to try to be virtuous). Alas, my lord, do not disregard this piece![22]

Though the logic and language of these passages are obtuse, one can trace P'i's argument with the use of a little imagination. In the preface to these admonitions the basic metaphor is established: that the mind is the lord of the body. P'i may have had the following passage from *Hsün-tzu* in mind here: "The ear, the eye, the nose, the mouth, and the body are, each in its own way, able to respond to external things and cannot be interchanged. These are called natural organs. The heart (mind) occupies the cavity in the center to control the five organs. This is called the natural ruler."[23] The analogy may also be intended to recall one or more passages from the *Great Learning.*[24] In the first two paragraphs of the "Admonition" itself P'i warns of the results of disagreement between mind (lord) and body (subject), and maintains that Shun's virtuous mind was made a subject to this disharmony, while the wicked mind of Chou Hsin was lord over it. The third paragraph seems to imply the Mencian idea that the people were more important than the ruler.[25] In a state (or a body) where this is not so, one has only Chou Hsin and his licentious subjects, and the chain of governmental (or physiological) command breaks down.

From P'i's attention to an ideal individual it may prove of interest to move to an examination of two of his biographical studies. His "Biography of Chao's Daughter" records only a single event, albeit the pivotal occurrence, in her life:

The woman née Chao was from Salt Mountain in Southside. Her father was a salt merchant who stole from the profits and didn't pay the tax collectors. The government had him apprehended and he, according to the law, was to die. The death warrant was issued and the carrying out of the sentence was to be in a matter of days. His daughter sought an interview with the Salt and Iron Envoy and in tears laid her case before him in court, saying, "When I was seven my mother died and my father illicitly stole from the official profits to clothe and feed me and to make my life more comfortable. Now father's crime has been completely revealed and I ought to receive the same punishment. If that is not permissible, could you pardon him? If you cannot, I beseech you to let me follow my father and be punished with him!"

The judge, Ts'ui Ch'ü of Ch'ing-ho,[26] felt that this was morally right and therefore commuted the death sentence. Miss Chao wept profusely and said, "My life is that which my father previously nourished, and which you, sir, have now rewarded. I plan to cut off my hair and give myself up to studying Buddhism to requite your virtuous deed." Then, since she considered that a woman's word was hardly to be trusted, she took a knife from her bosom and immediately cut off her ear, to certify her oath. Ts'ui was even more impressed with the morality of this and indeed spared her father's life.

Miss Chao took care of the injuries her father incurred during punishment until they were better and then took leave of him and went to a Buddhist temple to become a nun.

P'i Jih-hsiu says, "In ancient times those in danger who sought help and those in calamity who sought relief demonstrated their trustworthiness[27] first, but once their country or family was safe, they would summarily break their promise. But it is indeed filial to be like Miss Chao, a girl still wet behind the ears, risking death to save her father! She punished herself to forswear her words—this is trustworthiness! She grasped filial duty in order to set up trustworthiness, stepping high above her age, so pure that a beautiful gem would not measure up to her chastity, so fragrant that an orchid would not equal her cultivation. She is far removed from those in antiquity who sought help while in danger or relief in the face of calamity. The gentlemen of today, who don't stand by their integrity in difficult times and don't fulfill their promises in times of peace, how could they compare to Miss Chao who took punishment upon herself? Yes, those in the future who compile histories of women had better not forget her!"[28]

The violent adherence to trust (reminiscent of *hsia* or knight-errant ethics) espoused herein may seem barbaric to the modern reader. But even Confucian mores reflected the ephemeral social conditions of the ninth century—witness P'i's "Writings of a Recluse at Deer-Gate." It is in keeping, moreover, with the emperor-mind analogy of "On the Origin of the Self." In a milieu in which desperate measures were needed to save the empire, such acts as Miss Chao's self-mutilation are not surprising.

The narrative techniques in this piece show some influence from the contemporary school of rhetorical writers. Thus Miss Chao's background and argument are presented not in the summary of a narrator, but in her own words, which only adds somewhat indirectly to the trust the reader feels for her.

P'i's "Biography of Ho Wu" again returns to the concerns of Deer-Gate. The central incident of Ho's life is one which revolves about slander, flattery, and a feeling of moral indebtedness:

Ho Wu was a brave soldier of Shou prefecture.[29] Formerly, he was made general of the infantry and sent to guard Lin-huo Peak.[30] Mr. Yüeh, whose cognomen was Ch'uan, was a petty merchant who exploited so much that the people revolted. Discontented, the people were forced to make a formal complaint to the general. Wu went to him, and having upbraided him for inciting a riot, arrested him and put him in fetters. Waiting to square up accounts, Wu notified the prefect of Shou and asked for permission to

execute him. The clique of the man who had incited the disturbance, fear-
ing for their lives, slandered Wu in a plaint to the prefect. Moreover, they
said that Wu hadn't followed the prefect's orders, acting on his own, and
had killed people besides. The prefect of Shou was very fierce and could not
be opposed. If he learned of discontent among the people, even if it were
caused by a powerful colleague or a high officer, he always insulted and
killed the offenders. Now when he heard of Wu's offense, he was like a
mother tiger aroused, or an enraged viper injured; that he was about to do
someone mortal harm was clear. He ordered able-bodied soldiers to bind
Wu and bring him to his prefectural headquarters. Wu already was aware
that he could argue that he had acted rightly, but, knowing that there was
no avoiding that extreme fierceness of the prefect and that he was certain to
be wronged, he contentedly awaited death. When he arrived (at the headquarters), the prefect was in a rage and upbraided Wu for his errors. Wu
was skilled at replying in a flattering way, and his figure was imposing, thus
he tossed the stone.[31] He related the affair of how he had been wronged.
The prefect especially liked this sort, and, overturning the verdict, released
him, degrading him one rank. Wu said, "That I don't return beneath the
earth today, is truly your conferment. I owe you my life."

Not long thereafter highwaymen arose on all sides of a county seat in
Shou called Ts'ung-yang,[32] and the city was in great danger; Wu appealed
to the prefect, "Now is truly the time to fulfill my debt."

The prefect enlisted him and restored his former rank. He received
orders to be second in command, and, directing one flank of the army,
entered Ts'ung-yang by means of a shortcut. Unexpectedly, they were
ambushed en route by the bandits, who emerged from the screen of a
clump of trees. The soldiers all fled terrified, leaving Wu alone to fight to
the death.

P'i Jih-hsiu says, "Wu was slandered and his punishment was unde-
served, let alone his death! For those without the heart of Wu, even if they
would have escaped death, they could not have been free from resentment.
How could they have been moved to give up their lives? Alas! When the
gentlemen of old encountered slander while serving a superior, or were
disgraced in the line of duty, those who would have certainly angrily taken
reprisals, to the point of breaking up families and destroying states, if they
had been spared by their lord, are too numerous to mention! Of the thirty-
six lords whose murders are recorded in the *Spring and Autumn Annals*,
there must have been instances which came about in just this way. Wu,
though only a soldier, alone had this kind of heart. It's a shame that, among
the gentlemen of today, I don't know of any who would have this resolve if
they were slandered or disgraced. Wu though only a soldier . . . !"[33]

Here the ethics certainly incorporate much more of the *hsia* war-
rior than the Confucian gentleman. Ho Wu's nonchalance in the

face of execution, his sense of debt, and his anxiousness to ride into a
rebel-held area, all reflect this. The lack of any reference to Confucian precepts (even the allusions to the *Spring and Autumn Annals*
cannot be considered Confucian in this context) illustrates the
pragmatic side of P'i, something he undoubtedly hoped to illustrate
(especially to the prefect of Shou who seems to have patronized
P'i[34]) to his colleagues in this examination-eve composition.

Aside from the practical relations between men which P'i
discussed in these biographies, the cosmological ties between
heaven and man, a concern of many earlier T'ang classical scholars,
interested him as well, as "Casting Doubt on a Lightning Punishment" illustrates:

In a village called Huang-hua in P'eng-i County there was a peasant
named Feng whose lands were so extensive that his own ox couldn't completely plow them, so that he hired other oxen to augment its strength.
Feng's unscrupulousness was a model for the entire village to imitate.
When he obtained another ox, he employed it all day and returned it at
night, whipped it to plow through the burning bright of day and flogged it to
hoe in the dark obscurity of night, not giving it a rest, until it appeared to be
at its limit. One day all of a sudden a bolt of lightning discharged abruptly
from the mountains, striking Feng dead.

P'i Jih-hsiu says, "The lightning punishment Heaven bestowed on Feng
was justified by his unscrupulousness. The people's livelihood is based on
no more than their successes in agriculture. All that they can't do is done by
the strength of domestic animals. Thus Heaven's protection of the oxen
protects as well the destiny of the people, and this is only proper! Now Feng
was overtaxing their strength and Heaven struck him down with lightning.
In the case of those worthless youths of Yen and Chao who bludgeoned oxen
for private enjoyment, or boiled them to sell at the market, the law was not
able to subdue them,[35] punishments were not able to frighten them. If
Heaven wanted to preserve oxen, why wasn't a bolt of lightning sent down
on them as punishment? Thus I'm not sure if Feng's death was the working
of Heaven and Earth."[36]

The attempt to explain logically this event, which could readily be
accepted in the traditional post-Han Confucian conception of
natural disasters as a means through which Heaven reacted to man's
errors, represents the movement in the T'ang away from the
superstitious "intermediaries" of the post-Han era toward the age of
classical Chinese thought. It reflects, too, contemporary late-T'ang
logical developments. P'i views the divine execution in ethical terms

as "justified." Oxen, as P'i notes, were a valued possession and essential to the agriculture upon which Chinese society is grounded. Yet the entire role of Heaven as an active participant in man's fate is thrown into question by the final uncertainty as to whether the impetus behind the lightning is divine or merely natural (earthly— from the mountains and of a less than supernatural origin).

This denial of divine intervention was engendered no doubt by the miserable political environment in which P'i lived. It was difficult to envision a world in which an omnipotent Heaven would punish or rectify injustice, since there was so much injustice. Thus, P'i developed a theory of indirect heavenly influence upon man, through a sage or his writings, and expressed these ideas most concisely in his "On the Origin of Moral Influence":

Someone said, "The moral influence of the sages was begun with the Three August Rulers,[37] perfected with the Five Emperors,[38] and established in the era of Confucius during the Chou dynasty. Its content is the Way, the power, humanity, and morality. Its forms are the books of poetry, documents, rites, and music. Among those who have served as kings for myriad generations, there has not yet been one who would change this and yet still have right principles on his side. Only when one comes to the Eastern Han did the teachings of the Western Regions (Buddhism) first flow through China. Why is it that these people, whose entire clans inspired respect, who exhausted their wealth in bestowing aid, whose sons left fathers, whose husbands went from their spouses, who, muddled and stupid, emulated their (Buddhist) customs, who trod through their doors, were as unstoppable as if all the rivers were overflowing? Has not the so-called moral influence of the sages been termed 'influencing the people'? Those who understand influence today are only those from the Western Regions. If there is someone who speaks of the influence of the sages, everyone considers him stupid. Doesn't that mean that the influence of the sages doesn't even attain the level òf those from the Western Regions?"

(I) replied, "Heaven is not (able) to repress disorder, (for it does) not produce a sage generation after generation. (Yet) its Way *(tao)* is preserved in words, and its teachings persist in literature. If there is opposition to its words, or action contrary to its teachings, this is then a crime. 'Among the ancients Yang Chu and Mo-tzu blocked the road; the words of Mencius then broke it open and enlarged upon it.'[39] Therefore, if one has had a Duke of Chou and a Confucius, but must have then a Yang Chu and a Mo-tzu, it is simply essential to have a Mencius. Today in the teachings of those from the Western Regions who have built foundations and deepened their springs, things are greatly more chaotic than Yang or Mo caused them to be! If these kinds of people become gentlemen among us, where does that leave *Mencius?* After one thousand generations, there has only been one Gentleman from Ch'ang-li (Han Yü) to bare his arms and stare angrily [at the Buddhists]; among thousands of people, only he vilified them. Although his words are circulated, he has not won people over to his Way. If among those who dress in the robes of great officers, every generation had a Gentleman from Ch'ang-li, then I would regard them as like Mencius [i.e., continuing the orthodox line]. Suppose that all the people of the world were like the people of Chieh; even if there were one citizen of Yao to attend to them, could his goodness transform the evil of a Chieh populace? Thus those who have their hearts in the Way are Yao people. But alas, the officers of today follow the depraved in order to manage the masses, grasp onto disorder to rule the empire. Their worthiness is honorable, but in seeking the degenerate they go against moral influence. Isn't this a sad state of affairs? A sad state of affairs!"[40]

The tension of this work in isolation seems to be provided by the struggle of the late T'ang Confucianists with the Buddhists. When one views the piece in the larger context of P'i's entire prose concept, it becomes clear that beneath the obligatory denigrations of the Buddhists, P'i has recognized that they alone understood "moral influence" in his day. Since it was inconceivable that the teachings of the Sages were not the equal of those from the "Western Regions," the fault must lie with the means of communication rather than with the message: "If there is someone who speaks of the influence of the sages, everyone considers him stupid." It seems that P'i is acknowledging the superiority of Buddhist oral proselytization. He notes that although the teachings of the Way "persist in literature *(wen)*," the Way itself is "preserved in words *(yen)*." In other words, the Way is kept current by oral interpretation *(yen)* of the classical corpus *(wen)*. The association of words and teaching, again oral, underscores this. Besides, the appeal to the orations of Mencius, and to Mencius's importance as someone who explicated the teachings of the Duke of Chou and Confucius, illustrates clearly that P'i felt that the powerful prose of a writer who could effectively wrangle with the specious Buddhist barkers was needed. The implied candidate for this weighty responsibility of carrying on Han Yü's attacks is no doubt P'i himself.[41]

Beyond the ideological conflict of this era was the physical struggle for the empire between the members of the aristocracy. The avaricious nature of this class and the resultant chaos among the populace are depicted in P'i's "A Reading of *The Strategies of Ssu-ma*":

In ancient times those who won the empire did so using people's hearts. Today those who win the empire do so using people's lives. T'ang and Yü esteemed humaneness, and the people under Heaven followed and made them emperors. Can this not be said to be "Winning the empire using people's hearts"? Han and Wei esteemed political power, drove their "children" [i.e., their people] beneath sharp swords, and struggled for every inch of land in a hundred battles. They ascended from the gentry class to the feudal caste. From among this feudal caste, they became emperors. Without armies, they inspired no awe; without battles, they acquired no fealty. Can this not be said to be "Winning the empire using people's lives"? Thereupon, this was developed into an art. An art which, the more refined it becomes, the more people will be killed. Strategy which, the more effective it becomes, the more extreme the damage it does. Alas, this is certainly not humaneness either! Those sincere and honest sorts don't dare to treasure their lives, firstly because they are in dread of punishment, and secondly because they covet rewards. The people in their relation to the lord are like children (to their parents). How is this different from a father desiring to slay his children, at first by deceiving them with authority, and then by enticing them with profit?
   "Mencius said, 'There are men who say "I am expert at military formations, I am expert at waging war." This is a grave crime.' "[42]
   If a lord deals with the people so [i.e., considers war to be a crime], though he may not win any land, I shall consider him a man of noble character.[43]

The Strategies of Ssu-ma (Ssu-ma fa) is an ancient five-chapter manual written by Ssu-ma Jang-chü (fl. 600 B.C.) which claimed that a state could not be ruled by Confucian virtues, but only through military force. P'i attempts to assail the moral improprieties of such a theory. Besides the overt reference to the criminal nature of war,[44] the basic theme of winning the empire by winning the people's hearts is also from *Mencius:* "There is a way to win the Empire; win the people and you will win the Empire. There is a way to win the people; win their hearts and you will win the people."[45] But P'i goes even one step further to claim that even without gaining land, a man who gains the hearts of the people is a "man of noble character." Within this argument, moreover, is the interesting observation that the ninth-century landowners were not of classical, but of Han provenance, and that they were ascended from lower social levels. Underlying this may even be the implied assertion that the founder of this aristocracy, Liu Pang (d. 195 B.C.), was himself a peasant. And finally, the concern with land grabbing seems to point again to a problem of the times—the accumulation of lands by the newly founded manors.

Not only the methods of gaining power, but also the proper behavior of those in power comes under P'i's scrutiny, as illustrated in the first of his "Ten Essays Resolving Doubtful Passages in the *Spring and Autumn Annals*":

> With regard to Chao Tun "murdering his lord" and Chü P'u "killing his father," the *Spring and Autumn Annals* clearly writes of their errors. How is it then that when Kung-tzu Wei of Ch'u murdered his lord Duke Hsi, and when the people of Ch'i murdered their lord Duke Tao, each was announced as having died of illness, and the *Spring and Autumn Annals* always recorded it by "[so and so] died"?
>
> It is said, "In a person's life the most important things are heaven and earth, the next are lord and father." If lord and father can be murdered, then there truly is no heaven and earth. This is the most loathsome thing for a living man and is a huge disgrace for a man of great discrimination. This is the reason that it is said in the *History of the Han*,[46] "Ruling or marrying one's mother are those things which the Sages did not record."[47]
>
> Chao Tun "returned without punishing the offender," so Tung Hu called it murdering his lord;[48] Chü P'u with his treasure came fleeing [to Lü from Chü], so Li Ko called it murdering his father.[49] With regard to these two, their guile was already known, and Confucius merely wrote them up acknowledging this knowledge. Those three rebels, however, murdered their lords, announcing that they died of illness. Confucius could not be deceived; that he wrote based on the announcement was because he could not bear to record [such atrocities]. Therefore, his sense of shame, and his punishments (for these three), lie in his not bearing to record [their atrocities]. As to those thirty-six in the *Spring and Autumn Annals* who murdered their lords, the rest of the rebels also were written up according to the announcement.[50]

The attention to the *Spring and Autumn Annals* is a tradition among the new critical scholars of the T'ang.[51] Many of P'i's predecessors, however, advocated supplanting the traditionally accepted commentary, the *Tso-chuan*, by another exegesis (often the *Kung-yang chuan*). P'i's approach is to reexamine the doubtful passages and to try and justify them. In the questionable passage above, Confucius has named two men, Chao Tun and Chü P'u, murderers, although

Chao was only guilty in a technical sense. He left his lord, whose tyrannical and immoral behavior had made him a likely target for an assassin. Chü, moreover, was but carrying out the will of the people and adhering to the unwritten law of primogeniture in executing his father. Confucius then failed to note that Kung-tzu Wei and Tzu-ssu (not Confucius's grandson, but another man) murdered their lords. P'i's explanation for this, that Confucius was unable to record crimes as horrible as regicide and patricide, and that by following the official report of death he avoided shame while implying criticism (the punishment of a bad name), is at first glance unconvincing. But it may be more easily understood when one recalls P'i's subtle dealings with a number of potential patrons with less than arrantly pure moral reputations.

Indeed, P'i's own reputation declares that his prose corpus is made up of historical and ethical discursions. Even his *fu* (prose-poems), written no doubt in preparation for the civil service examinations, are of a moralistic tone. There is one group of texts, however, written in imitation of the patriarch of Chinese literature, Ch'ü Yüan, which takes exception. In this unique belletristic series, P'i explores the possibilities of withdrawal from a society in need of reform. His "Sorrowful Journey" is typical:

> Lotus as a shift, and mugwort as a cloak;
> Fragrant plants as a short coat, and marsh grass
>   a scent-pouch;
> Stopping my oars by the banks of the Li,
> Halting my paddle by the brink of the Hsiang.
> 5 Grief would not be grief, but that I've recently
>   left my country;
> Resentment would not be resentment, but that we
>   must long for one another.
> . . . .
> Since there is no one to recognize me,
> 20 Why should I be of a mind to feel resentful and
>   sigh?
> Withdrawing without explaining my despair,
> Coming forward as if I knew no shame.
> The cold cicada is resentful and silent,
> The old trees shiver amid empty branches.
> 25 I bemoan my soul not being able to return,
>   And passing its life for a thousand seasons here
>   by the Hsiang.[52]

Although P'i had not been in exile as he wrote this piece, he probably took on the exile-pose during his sojourn in the Yangtze River Basin during the early 860s. This lament imitates the "Encountering Sorrow" in its imagery and theme, and again bears at least the suggestion that as P'i's emotional life is similar to that of the great master, Ch'ü Yüan, his political problems with a corrupt court parallel those of ancient Ch'u.

III P'i's Prose and Neo-Confucianism: Concluding Remarks

The concerns of P'i's prose writings prove in many ways prophetic. The inroads of Buddhism, the concern with the more mystical and metaphysical aspects of the Confucian canon, and the politico-social changes of the T'ang-Sung transition mark P'i's work as a stepping stone in the evolution of Neo-Confucianism. Yet the path he prepared was not followed, for early Sung philosophers rejected the idea that the Confucian tradition alone could provide the material to revitalize itself. In accepting Taoist and Buddhist concepts, they cause most of the late T'ang "disciples" of Han Yü and Li Ao (772–841), who had first advocated Confucian reform, to be considered outdated and reactionary. Although key terms and concepts can be traced back through Sung thinkers to P'i's corpus, it is more likely that they were derived from the same canonical texts that P'i used, rather than from P'i's works themselves. Nevertheless, it is noteworthy that P'i was as interested in a cross-section of philosophical solutions to the disorder of a kindred era, the late Warring States Period (such as *The Strategies of Ssu-ma*), as he was in any particular philosophical school. And, as a man from the periphery of the social groups which had defined and transmitted classical texts and knowledge for so long, his ideas are of significance in viewing the intellectual history of the important transitional era in which he lived.

CHAPTER 4

From Tradition to Experiment: Poetry

I *Introduction*

BEFORE examining P'i's poetry written in the period prior to his passing the examinations in 867, some comments on the state of the art in the late ninth century may be of use. This discussion is not merely intended to review the findings of the literary historians who pronounce the late T'ang period (*ca.* 835–907) one in which the prosodic limits of new-style poetry had been reached, resulting in the overflow lines of the *tz'u* (lyric), nor to reiterate the tenets of the major camps of the era, Chia Tao and his followers versus Chang Chi's "school." It will also examine the coeval methods of composition and of comprehension, to the extent that they may still be determined.

With regard to composition, the late T'ang is an era in which wholesale incorporation of phrases and even complete lines from earlier poets began to become more and more commonplace. A well known example might be the following line from Lu Kuei-meng's "White Lotus": "Without emotion, without regret, who sees?"[1] Lu has then been praised by modern scholars for this line without their realizing its provenance:[2] it was taken verbatim from a verse by Li Ho.[3] Similarly, one can sense the shallowness of the abilities of the twentieth-century sinophile vis-à-vis the T'ang reader by comparing the following prose-poems:

Prose-poem on a Louse
Li Shang-yin

First the vital force and it is impregnated,
Then the egg and it takes physical form.
Early-morning ducks, dew-covered geese,
Don't know of its birth.

5 Your task is only to gnaw,
   Yet you don't gnaw well;
   Surrounded by odor you multiply,
   Treading on incense[4] you reach your end.[5]

On first reading the poem seems straightforward and mundane—a
piece written in preparation for the examinations, perhaps, and in
the tendency which continues in the Sung dynasty of trying to make
the unaesthetic aesthetic. Yet when one serendipitously comes
across Lu Kuei-meng's sequel, it becomes obvious that "close reading" is an invention of neither the French lycée nor the American
New Critic:

Sequel to the "Prose-poem on a Louse" with a Preface
Lu Kuei-meng

When I read Mr. Yü-hsi's [Li Shang-yin's] "Prose-poem on a Louse," I
sighed in admiration of its nearing Yen and avoiding Chih. Yet it seemed as
if he had never known a louse. I wrote the "Sequel to the 'Prose-poem on a
Louse' " to set things right:

Though the clothes are black, to keep to white;
Though the hair is white, to hold to black.
Not changing because of external appearances—
This is the constancy of virtue

A petty man follows the times,
And has to change his colors.
To abandon the lean and pursue the fat,
Is just the foible[6] of the louse.[7]

The first quatrain of Lu's sequel refers to the *Tao-te ching*, 28:

He who knows the male and keeps to the female
Becomes the ravine of the world.
Being the ravine of the world,
He will never depart from eternal virtue,
But returns to the state of infancy.
He who knows the white [alternately explained as "glory"]
   and yet keeps to the black ["humility"],
Becomes the model for the world.
Being the model for the world,
He will never deviate from eternal virtue . . .[8]

Thus the allusion is appropriate in an argument for a humble, mean being like the louse. But more importantly one notes in the preface the reference to Yen Hui, Confucius's favorite disciple who died young after a life marked by poverty and austerity,[9] and to Liu-hsia Chih, an ancient brigand representing the ultimate in greed, violence, and luxuriant living.[10] One sees this echoed in line 7, where the "fat" may be Chih, and the "lean," Hui. But strikingly the significance of this entire prose-poem for the contemporary reader is the key it provides to understanding Li Shang-yin's work: *hui*, translated above as "to be surrounded by," and *chih*, "to tread on," can now be seen to refer to Yen Hui and Liu-hsia Chih. A revised version of this last section would read:

> Your job is only to gnaw,
> Yet you don't gnaw well;
> In Yen Hui's odor you multiply,
> On Liu-hsia Chih's incense you reach your end.

The louse "doesn't gnaw well" because it preys on a good man, Yen Hui, but is repelled from a rascal like Liu-hsia Chih, owing to the latter's luxuriant toilet. For readers as carefully trained in the classics as the T'ang literati were, such an oversight would have been unthinkable. But despite the discrepancy between current knowledge of the traditional corpus versus that held during the T'ang, something which can be made up for in part through a careful use of modern reference aids, one should also note the delight with which both Li Shang-yin and Lu Kuei-meng manipulate their language and their readers. In this a modern critic can take heart, for despite the danger of occasionally reading too much into a text,[11] one can see that verbal play was very much a part of both the composition and the comprehension of literature during the T'ang.

Turning to the prosodic developments of the ninth century, one might note the predominance of the seven-word line new-style poem. The new- or modern-style verse *(chin-t'i shih)* is primarily a development of T'ang dynasty poets.[12] It is distinguished from old- or ancient-style verse by its verbal parallelism and its carefully defined prosodic patterns based on the natural tonality of Chinese. Put simply, there were four tones in the Chinese spoken during the T'ang. These tones were classified into two categories for use in poetry: the even tone, and the other three "uneven" (rising, going, and entering) tones. There are two types of new-style verse, the *lü-shih* or "regulated poem" of eight lines, and the *chüeh-chü*, a four-line form. Within the lines themselves, the last three words (of the five- or seven-word lines) function as a comment on the topic presented in the first two (or four) words of the line. Since the prosodic regulations are more important than their syntactical or grammatical counterparts, "texture," the local interaction of words in a work of art, gains in importance. The language is compact and the result is often ambiguity. Because of the semantic and prosodic parallelism, however, the couplet is the basic unit. Beginning with the first couplet of the poem, each couplet functions as commentary to the preceding lines (the first couplet to the title), and topic for the following lines. The final two lines are unique in that they generally present a proposition, and are intellectual, rather than emotional or sensory, in their appeal. Yet the new-style poem, and especially the seven-word-line variety, was a highly valued form, as Hu Chen-heng (1569–1644/45) noted centuries ago:

Why is it that seven-word old-style poetry is a bit easier (to compose) than five-word old-style, and yet seven-word regulated poetry is more difficult than five-word regulated? In five-word old-style poetry ideas are easily run together, so that those who haven't studied it in depth find it difficult to bring a poem together. The style of the seven-word old variety is crystal clear, so that those who are even slightly gifted with talent and emotion can readily give poetic expression to them. The regulations of five-word regulated are simple and minimal, so that even those who have some slight skill can easily become proficient in their composition. The prosodic rules of a seven-word regulated poem are numerous and complicated, so that even though one may have talent which is vast and all-encompassing, it may prove difficult to select just the right words to fit the patterns.[13]

By the late ninth century, however, the possibilities of this form had nearly been exhausted. Hu Chen-heng again summarizes this development:

The seven-word line regulated poem of the T'ang underwent a transformation between the fine labors of Tu Shen-yen (*ca.* 648–*ca.* 708) and Shen Ch'üan-ch'i (*ca.* 656–714) in founding (the form), and Ts'ui Hao (704–754) and Li Po (701–763), who for a time brought out the old themes, [other poets and the transformations they induced are described] . . . and P'i Jih-hsiu and Lu Kuei-meng's stuffing it with ancient stories . . . are all changes difficult to entirely record. The more the regulated form ran along, the more it declined, until with the T'ang throne it announced its end.[14]

Nevertheless, rather than reject this jaded but complex form for one of the newer alternatives (such as *tz'u*), P'i Jih-hsiu followed the contemporary trend and composed over half of his (extant) corpus in this form, as the following chart illustrates:[15]

New Style	Regulated verse	Five-word line	94	
		Seven-word line	137	233
		Six-word line	2	
	Quatrain (*chüeh-chü*)	Five-word line	12	60
		Seven-word line	48	
Old Style		Four-word line	9	
		Five-word line	63	73
		Seven-word line	1	
Miscellaneous				40
Linked Verse				8
			Total	414

Thus P'i Jih-hsiu's significance lies not in pioneering a new form, but in stubbornly exploring a medium which many considered already threadbare. His experiments alone gainsay some importance. In addition, the very size of his corpus, although not the largest of the period,[16] is noteworthy, for it represents little more than a single year's output.

II *Early Poetry*

Those extant poems dating prior to P'i's arrival in Soochow in the late 860s are primarily didactic. Once more Hu Chen-heng provides a succinct appraisal of the two periods of P'i's work:

In the poetry P'i Jih-hsiu wrote prior to his passing the examinations he esteemed the unadorned and the rough without variegation. After the

examinations, while sojourning along the Sung-ling River, in works like his
Great Lake pieces, his talented brush opened horizons and was filled with
wonderfully captivating lines. Carving out images and piling up allusions
like fallen petals in his regulated poetry, one could chant it without understanding a sound. His weakness was putting his brush to paper so that words
preceded feeling and there was neither wind nor bone[17] to act as a frame.[18]

The terms "unadorned" and "rough" were often used to describe
the poetry of Han Yü, and several critics have pointed to an affinity
between the two poets. Perhaps P'i's "Nine Great Songs, number
one" recalls some of Han Yü's four-word-line verse:[19]

> Fiery, so fiery is the brilliant sun,
> All at once lovely in the heavens.
> Its brightness coming forth in proper order,
> Like the king going out.
>
> 5 Fiery, so fiery is the brilliant sun,
> All at once entering into the earth.
> Its darkness, its purity,
> Like the king returning.
>
> Going out there are the dragon banners,
> 10 Coming back there are the girdle pendants.
> Not at a gallop or a trot,
> Only with care, only with reserve.
>
> Going out there is excellent counsel,
> Coming back the rules for within the palace and harem;
> 15 Yes, those ministers and people are
> Models through which the king may command respect.[20]

This verse was one of a series written to amend the *Rites of Chou*.
One detects herein only an implied didacticism. Since the poem is
an imitation of the paeans *(sung)* of the *Book of Poetry*, it is lent the
moral associations of this respected corpus. The ability to recreate a
work which in diction, prosody, and tone seems faithful to the ancient paeanic tradition is of greater significance. The lines are all
four words in length, and the rhyme scheme (following contemporary T'ang pronunciation) is xaxa bcbc xdxd. Both are modeled on
the prosody of the paean. The first lines of the first two stanzas are
hsing (motifs), which commonly introduced a theme in the ancient
odes. As one scholar has described *hsing*, its "elements bear up the
structure of each poem where they appear, as they start or reinforce

the rhythm, establish the sound pattern, and set the mood."[21] They also lead to associations beyond the literal meaning of the poem.[22] Thus although the technique here is ancient, the associations and the theme itself, depicting the king in terms of the brilliant sun, belong also to the T'ang. The language is based upon the *Rites of Chou:* the last two words of line 3 are used to describe the "coming forth in proper order" of the palace ladies when the king retires at night.[23] The tenth and twelfth lines again suggest palace women and the ritual pertaining to the king's relations with them. They have seen him off in the morning and now welcome him home at dusk. The final stanza is based on an allusion to the "Chün ch'en" section of the *Book of Documents:* ". . . *going out and coming in,* seek the judgment of your people about them [i.e., the plans of the government]; and where there is general agreement, exert your own powers of reflection. When you have any good plans or counsels, enter and lay them before your sovereign in his palace."[24]

Thus, though the poem is but an exercise, it illustrates several of P'i's early literary concerns. The developed, but clearly stated metaphors are, like the vocabulary, archaic. The prosodic simplicity is typical of much of P'i's early poetry. This poem in particular exhibits most probably the influence of Yüan Chieh (719–772), whom, as P'i related in his preface to the *Literary Marsh*, was one of his models. The "Nine Great Songs" were intended in the *Rites of Chou* as those which accompanied the emperor's departure and return. P'i's reconstructions are as well part of the literary movement which sought to return beyond commentaries directly to the classics, and thereby to influence the ruler by providing him a relevant, yet relic, exemplar. The particular emphasis on restraint regarding relations with women would have been especially apt during the 860s when the licentious I-tsung sat on the throne.

A more obstrusively didactic series of poems was P'i's "Three Poems of Shame." The third of this series, together with the preface, is presented here:

Preface

In the *ping-hsü* year [866] the southern bank of the Huai River was plagued by locusts and a drought. P'i Jih-hsiu had lived in a small villa in the eastern part of the prefecture. After failing to pass the examinations, he returned there and saw those of the Ying River region populace who were moving out of the region filling the roads and blocking the paths, to the

point that fathers were rejecting their children and husbands renouncing
their wives. As they moved along, they wept. When they stood still, they
begged. Setting out in the morning, by evening they were dead. Damn!
Heaven and earth are truly inhumane! In Master P'i's mountain home there
is a suit of clothes on a hanger and food in the kettle. He sleeps late and by
evening is still full. In the morning he is joyful and at dusk he rejoices. What
ability does he have that he alone among the people of the Ying can enjoy
this? Is it that heaven and earth have deserted them? Thus ashamed and
unable to comfort himself he composed this poem in condolence for them.

> In the *ping-hsü* year of our Emperor,
> Many people were starving on the south bank of the Huai.
> In this area, at the Ying's watersmeet,
> They were moving as if strung in lines.
> 5   Husband and wife died looking at one another,
> Abandoning even babes in their arms.
> Brothers separated from one another,
> Leaving home as if at wit's end!
> A piece of gold in exchange for radishes,
> 10   The best silks could fetch only water chestnuts.
> In the deserted villages birds use gravestones as trees,
> About empty homes wild flowers form hedges.
> Children gnaw at grasses and roots,
> And lean on mulberry trees, too weak to stand.
> 15   The white-haired die by the roadside,
> Pillowed on one another, all heartbroken.
> Now I understand the teachings of the sages
> That the goodness of the people depends on situations like this.
> Such cruelty can take away people's love,
> 20   Such desolation can snatch away their compassion.
> How could he who is to shepherd them [i.e., the ruler]
> Have a policy for dealing with what is involved here?
> What sort of man am I,
> With several acres by a clear stream?
> 25   After writing those pieces which caused my
>   failure in the examinations,
> My whole family can still enjoy life.
> For breakfast there is wheat gruel,
> Arising at dawn we have thin robes.
> My person is fed and warm,
> 30   My family has nothing to complain about.
> Though we have several acres of fields,
> My hands don't hold a hoe.
> In this year though there've been deaths from the bad harvest,

Our kitchen hasn't had to do away with breakfast.
35 What road has led to this?
I have an enlightened gentleman who understands.
He fed me with food befitting a marquis,
Clothed me in clothes of the same sort.
When I returned he helped me with money and fine
   garments,
40 And enabled me to serve my parents.
I examine myself and shame before the people of the Ying—
How could I not have tried to improve my virtues?
Because of this I am moved by his understanding of me,
And weep in vain the whole day long.[25]

In this poem P'i takes the pose of the empathetic Confucian supported by a patron and living amidst one of the frequent disasters of
the late ninth century. The poem is almost formulaic for the first
twenty lines. Illustrating the severity of a famine by citing inflation-
ary prices (lines 9–10), for example, is typical of such verse. The
following couplet, which depicts the devastation from a point of
view other than man's (the birds find gravestones more numerous
than trees), is strikingly original, though. Lines 17–18 refer clearly
to Mencian principles. They may allude to specific "teachings" such
as: "Nowadays, the means laid down for the people are sufficient
neither for the care of parents nor for the support of wife and children. In good years life is always hard, while in bad years there is no
way of escaping death. Thus simply to survive takes more energy
than the people have. What time can they spare for learning about
rites and duty?"[26] Or:

"In years of bad harvest and famine," answered Mencius, "close on a
thousand of your people suffered, the old and the young being abandoned
in the gutter, the able-bodied scattering in all directions, yet your granaries
were full and there was failure on the part of your officials to inform you of
what was happening. This shows how callous those in authority were and
how cruelly they treated the people. . . . It is only now that the people have
had an opportunity of paying back what they received. You should not bear
them any grudge. Practice benevolent government and the people will be
sure to love their superiors and die for them."[27]

If not specific allusions, P'i's lines certainly embody in general Mencius's concept of benevolent government as the basis of the well-
being of the people and the strength of the state. Even the imagery

and diction of this poem parallel passages in *Mencius*. Yet this reading is seriously undermined by lines 21–22. According to *Mencius*, the ruler should have a "policy for dealing with" this distress: benevolent rule. The very word policy itself *(shu)* is primarily a Legalist term. Burton Watson explains it as follows: ". . . the concept of *shu*—policies, methods, or arts of governing . . . the ruler, who is the author of law and outside and above it, must be guided by a different set of principles. These principles constitute his *shu*, the policies and arts which he applies in wielding authority and controlling the men under him."[28] P'i's use of it here may be an attempt to reduce the responsibility of his superiors and to attribute the blame to heaven (see the preface—"Heaven and earth are truly inhumane! "). This would coincide with the remaining lines which portray the kindness of his patron and P'i's shame at not being able to relieve the suffering about him. Thus this verse marks either P'i's willingness to compromise his principles when faced with the necessity to chastise someone who might be able to promote his career, or the Legalist overtones which scholars in the People's Republic of China claim to detect in P'i's corpus.[29]

In another view of peasant life P'i takes the reader to the West-border Mountain located near Hu-chou in modern Chekiang:[30]

"A Fisherman's Family at the Western-border Mountain Quai"

'Neath a white-silk kerchief, hair like silken thread,
Docilely leaning against the roots of a maple
 as I sit fishing the jetty.
The second son's wife has gone to Mulberry Hamlet
 to pick leaves,
A young boy's returned from Sandy Market having
 bought rain cloaks.
Since the rain the water shields polish drifting
 boats smooth,
After spring the sea perch are so fat they sink the hooks.
Beneath West-border Mountain I spent the whole day—
 an outsider,
Envying them across the waves, I couldn't bring
 myself to leave.[31]

The mention of Western-border Mountain would certainly take the T'ang reader back to a series of five lyrics *(tz'u)* on fishermen composed by Chang Chih-ho *(ca.* 730–*ca.* 810).[32] The setting is thus topical. A fisherman pursues one of the few traditional Chinese life-styles which were considered to allow a man to live at harmony with nature. The poet seems to be a participant in this family and its life-style. He wears a white-silk kerchief, symbolic of the recluse,[33] and sits fishing. He is familiar with the family's comings and goings. Yet in the final couplet, one learns that he is in fact neither a member of the family nor a true fisherman. The realization lends a tension to all the preceding lines. The details observed, such as the rain-soaked weeds lending their sheen of moisture to passing boats, are seen as in keeping with the "outsider's" status of the poet. But one now suspects, remembering the topical nature of the setting, that the industrious second son's wife of the third line, and perhaps the entire poem, is a formulaic construction (she and a younger, carefree sister are often seen in *yüeh-fu* poetry). The overall impression becomes one of the "grass being greener." Passing boats seem to glisten (the original line is ambiguous—"smooth" may refer either to the water shields or to the boats; the translation is an attempt to maintain this ambiguity), the fish on their hooks are all fat. The poet admits he is an intruder, separated from these people not only by the waters between them. But he is also conscious of his advancing age (the "hair like silken thread" in line 1 refers to its whiteness) and perhaps longs for the idyllic life of this idealized family. The poem thus reflects once again the quandary in which P'i often finds himself: committed to the life of a civil servant, he still appreciates the purity and simple pleasures of the common people.

Still very much in touch with the common people are P'i's "Orthodox Music Bureau Ballads,"[34] a series of ten poems modeled on Yüan Chieh's twelve verses entitled "Propagating the Music Bureau Ballads."[35] The second of this series, "Lament of a Woman Acorngatherer," is similar to many of the New Music Bureau Ballads made popular by Po Chü-i and Yüan Chen in its harsh criticism of government corruption and its vivid depiction of the hardships of peasant life:

> Deep into autumn the acorns ripen,
> Scattering as they fall into the scrub on the hill.
> Hunched over, a hoary-haired crone
> Gathers them, treading the morning frost.
> 5 After a long time she's got only a handful,
> An entire day just fills her basket.

First she suns them, then steams them,
To use in making late winter provisions.
At the foot of the mountain she has ripening rice,
10   From its purple spikes a fragrance pervades.
Carefully she reaps, then hulls the grain,
Kernel after kernel like a jade earring.
She takes the grain to offer as government tax,
In her own home there are no granary bins.
15   How could she know that well over a picul of rice
Is only five pecks in official measurement?
Those crafty clerks don't fear the law,
Their greedy masters won't shun a bribe.
In the growing season she goes into debt,
20   In the off-season sends grain to government vaults.
From winter even into spring,
With acorns she tricks her hungry innards.
I've heard that T'ien Ch'eng-tzu,
By feigning benevolence, made himself a king.
25   Aah, meeting this old woman acorn-gatherer!
Tears come uncalled to moisten my robe.[36]

Although many of these ballads are based in hyperbole, the Japanese monk Ennin (793–864) reports that he encountered famine conditions in Shantung in the early 840s such that acorns were being eaten there.[37] The earring and fragrance of lines 10 and 12 may be intended to mock palace-poetry laments and to contrast the physical rigors of this peasant crone's existence with the psychological strains of the harem women. The allusion in the penultimate couplet to T'ien Ch'eng-tzu, who won the hearts of the people of the state of Ch'i by reducing the standard grain measure used in collected taxes,[38] but then shortly thereafter assassinated his lord and usurped the throne, may refer to some specific well-intended reformer of the period, or it may simply indicate the duplicity of a government in dealing with its subjects. By noting that benevolence, the basic Confucian principle of governing, can be feigned, P'i is perhaps again hinting at the necessity for Legalistic measures.

The fourth poem in this series, "Song of a Farmer," employs the technique of a peasant adversary overheard by the persona:

A peasant oppressed by sorrow and misery
Described his feelings to me:
"It's hard for a single farming man

To provide for ten out on campaign.
5 Why are the grains of the South and East
Transported by boat to the ruler's domain?
In the Yellow River the waters are like lightning,
And half of the load overturns and sinks.
If the adjuster or transport men profit in their service,
10 How dare we people criticize an official's gain?
Don't they farm along the Three Rivers' banks?
Don't they plow the Three Districts' plain?
How is it they don't cart off theirs
To supply the imperial troops in grain?"
15 Beautiful! That peasant's speech,
But how are we to carry this message to the end of
the king's road?[39]

Although here again are the standard complaints to be found in so
many of these ballads, P'i's specific reference to boats overturning
and to the dichotomy between the economic center in the Yangtze
delta area and the political hub at Ch'ang-an dates this work as
belonging to late T'ang. Indeed, in the works of early New Music
Bureau balladeers such criticism was usually mollified by directing
it at some past error or by avoiding specific references. But P'i
stresses especially the unfairness of the North's hegemony over the
South during his lifetime ("Three Rivers" and "Three Districts" are
both metonyms for the capital regions) and the unlikelihood that a
southern appeal could ever reach the "end of the king's road" far to
the north. The very simple vocabulary and imagery reflect the
straightforwardness of the appeal and its persona.

"Pity the Righteous Birds" is number eight in this series. It describes the fowl which had been hunted and presented as tribute
from the Mount Shang-yen area in modern Shensi:

On Mount Shang-yen are many righteous birds,
Righteous birds, truly lamentable!
Nesting precariously on peaks piled high,
Hidden midst the varnish-tree blossoms.
5 If a chick happens into its nest,
It will nurse it as if it were its own.
If another nest is seized,
It will throw itself into the same nets.
Merchants present them as tribute every autumn,
10 But why are they so prized after all?

Fattened on a diet of rice and millet,
Adorned with the splendor of embroidered silk.
Pitiable, this humane, dutiful fowl,
Sent to sport for a palace beauty,
15 I've heard of the nobility of the phoenix,
That its humanity and sense of duty merit praise;
The reason they are not caught,
Is probably because so few are born.[40]

To the theme of nature violated by the greed of the court P'i has
added the irony that the very birds seized by man are those which
exhibit the highest qualities man is capable of: the Confucian virtues
of humanity *(jen)* and moral duty or right *(i)*. The comparison with
the phoenix, the imperial emblem, may be intended to suggest a
comparison of these birds with scholar-officials who are brought to
court only for "sport," and to suggest that it is only the emperor's
status which has rescued him from a like fate. The passage (lines
5–9) depicting the strong feelings between a "family" of such fowl
may also be contrasted with humans facing such a crisis as described
in P'i's "Three Poems of Shame" above.

The final of these ten ballads again treats the theme of birds being
presented as tribute, but focuses primarily on the effects that such
demands have on the people of the region of Lung, a classical name
for the Kansu-Shensi border region:

"Lament for the People of Lung"

Lung Massif stands tens of thousands of feet;
Parakeets nest up on its peaks.
Pushed to lofty heights, then to further peril,
Even these mountains are not safe!
5 The simple folk of Lung
On hanging bridges seem to mount the sky;
Spying a nest up in the void,
Many fall as they scramble in quest.
Out of one hundred, not one bird is caught,
10 Of ten, nine men die in the attempt.
By the Lung River there are border troops,
Border troops not idle either;
Under orders to carry the carved cages
Straight to the entrance of the Golden Hall.
Those feathers are no treasure of themselves,
That tongue doesn't learn to speak of its own.

> Why make light of the lives of men
> To present these birds as objects of idle play?
> I have heard that the ancient sage-kings
> 20 Released all of their precious birds.
> But today these people of Lung
> Grieve unceasingly year after year.[41]

The trivial nature of the basis of this complaint coupled with the solemnity of P'i's criticism may seem unusual, almost ludicrous, to the modern reader. Yet in the context of these ten ballads, primarily appeals from regions not normally heeded by the central government,[42] the significance of the people of Lung's dilemma is enhanced. The point that mere predilections of the court may cause devastation in the provinces is well made here, and thus this final piece aptly summarizes this decagonal, poetic memorial.

Aside from the didactic pieces, however, some of P'i's early verse was of an occasional nature (as seen in chapter 1). The following "New Year's Eve in an Inn" illustrates this group of poems and serves as a viable transition to P'i's later poetry:

> In this far-reaching night, who can keep watch?
> A traveler's heart is not given to sleep.
> As I hung the lanterns it was still the old,
> But hearing horns, it's now the New Year!
> Coming out of the valley I sigh in vain at the late hour,
> Raising the cup I feel shame for my earlier life.
> At dawn as I bid farewell to the inn,
> Snow weeps in the wild-locust tree sky.[43]

Though an old-style poem, the language here is already more compressed and may foreshadow P'i's later work. The first binome in the poem, "far-reaching," for example, connotes the traditional ties of the New Year, the length of the winter just ending, the psychologically dilatory nature of this night of anticipation, as well as the mere physical passage of time. The close parallelism of lines 3–6 underlines the juxtaposition of the old and new years, and the lateness of the hour (to be understood metaphorically) versus P'i's "earlier life." The overall tone is optimistic, however. The images of lanterns hung high, horns, the persona emerging from a valley and raising his cup, and finally the dawn with its farewell to the old and the dark, prepare the powerful final figure of nature's cathartic ablution.

Even the point of view of the persona can be triangulated in these
closing lines. His head raised to his cup, his eyes catch the rays of
dawn, and, finally, as he sets off on his journey he sees the world
with his eyes still held high, as if the wild-locusts above him were
traced across the sky.

This poem, which bespeaks more the style of another native of
Hsiang-yang, Tu Mu (803–852), marks a departure from his early
Han Yü–influenced style and the themes taken from Po Chü-i. The
attention paid to prosody and imagery may serve to introduce P'i's
later verse.

III *Later Verse*

P'i Jih-hsiu's later verse, over three hundred poems, was composed primarily during the year he spent with Lu Kuei-meng in
Soochow (870). Most of this corpus is to be admired for its technical
felicities. One modern scholar has described their work as follows:
"[Lu and P'i'] almost completely broke open the restrictions of modern-style poetry. When we read their verse, although the tonal
structure is rough, it is as if they were principally pondering emotions and scenes in poetry, so that one senses that midst this rough-
ness, there is a tendency towards a carefreeness, and this is one of
the special characteristics of P'i and Lu."[44] Yet there are also particular aspects of the new milieu which especially attracted P'i.
Some were concerns that he had shown previously in his writing;
others were, like the landscape, novel.

A. *Antiquity*

Left more to leisure in Soochow, P'i's thoughts turned more and
more from present-day problems to the romance of the past. One
notes this already in a simple verse entitled "The Ancient Han
Pass," which P'i wrote en route southward:

> In rubble this ancient border fortress
> Can still guard the imperial capital.
> As a traveler of today passes by,
> He doesn't wait for the cocks to crow at dawn.[45]

The final line refers to the ancient practice of opening a pass only at
dawn. It may also sardonically recall the retainer of Lord
Meng-ch'ang (r. 319–*ca.* 301 B.C.) who saved his liege by imitating a

cock's crow causing the pass to open before emissaries of the King of
Ch'in could overtake them.[46] Thereby some contrasts between
China in the Warring States Period and the T'ang empire during the
late ninth century would be implied. Though the first line is a
realistic depiction of a ruin, it almost suggests the neglect of the
contemporary government toward military defense. The comparison to Meng-ch'ang's retainer, a man who had won the lord's favor
only with great difficulty, may be meant to emphasize P'i's unrecognized loyalty.

Many of the poems of this year depict the local history of the
Soochow region itself, such as his "Ancient Palace Tunes, Three
Verses, number one":

> Keeps and halls lean toward the bright moon,
> Jagged like the restless mountain peaks.
> The palace flowers unfold at midnight,
> They won't wait for the bells of dawn.[47]

Although ostensibly a verse complaining of the unattended flowers
—i.e., women—in the palace of Emperor Wu of the Ch'i dynasty
(the final line refers to bells installed in the Dawn Tower by the
emperor to warn him of the imminent dawn, since he could not hear
the normal means of marking time from the inner reaches of the
harem), the artistry is noteworthy. "Jagged" is more often an epithet
applied to city or palace skylines, and its use along with the comparison to "reckless" mountains hints at disorder in the palace. As
the keeps and halls seem to lean toward the moon, the palace
flowers open to the unnatural, *yin* luminary, unable to wait for the
Great Yang or sun. As unnatural as moonlight is to flowers, would be
the midnight rising of an immoderately large harem in which so
many women were neglected that they must have opened to other
sources of *yin*. In other words, without the love of the emperor,
they shared one another. The poem is tied by the textural relations
between the palace buildings and the mountains, the verb "to lean
toward" which might readily pair with flowers, the reckless peaks
and the equally desperate women, and the visual force of the moon
vis-à-vis the expected emasculated aural coming of the dawn.

By far P'i's greatest predilection was for the palaces of Wu where
the lovely Hsi Shih bewitched the king, Fu Ch'ai, and enabled Kou
Chien and the Yüeh armies to avenge an earlier defeat and conquer

Wu. Kuan-wa Kung (Belle Lodging Palace), the most famous of these residences, is the site of the following poem:

"Five *Chüeh-chü* Poems Longing for the Past at
Belle Lodging Palace, number one"

About glittering bowers a whirling fragrance
    descends upon Great Lake,
Until one morning mutinous troops ascend Ku-su
    Tower.
The King of Yüeh should feel great shame,
For simply using Hsi Shih to gain Wu by artifice.[48]

This short poem summarizes the story of Hsi Shih. The Belle Lodging Palace was built on Tien-shih shan (Inkwell Stone Mountain) southwest of modern Soochow by the King of Wu, Fu Ch'ai, for her. The strict parallelism of lines 1 and 2 divides the poem into two distinct couplets. The "glittering bowers" are those in which the palace women live. They provide an interesting foil for the rampaging enemy troops, especially since the original epithet used to describe these soldiers, *luan*, suggested confusion and disarray as well as rebellion. *Luan* also informs the reader that the persona's allegiance is to the state of Wu. "Whirling fragrance" is a well-chosen binome. Texturally it abets the connection between the pavilions and the troops which swarm about them, as well as intimating the reflections of the pavilions in the waters of the lake. "Break of dawn" heightens the sensuousness of the first line, adding darkness to the scented chambers of Hsi Shih. Since its literal force is "invading the dawn," it falls into place cleverly in line 2 and carries the troops through the natural barrier of sunrise to the steps of the Ku-su Terrace. There some years earlier (in 496 B.C.) Kou Chien had defeated Fu Ch'ai's father, Ho Lü, and mortally wounded him in the process.[49] The tower itself had been built by Ho Lü in 510 B.C. and could be seen from a distance of nearly one hundred miles. It symbolized the revival of Wu under Fu Ch'ai. Line 3 alludes to the King of Yüeh's ascetic life-style after his defeat by Fu Ch'ai, and contrasts it to the pleasures of Fu Ch'ai's court, the primary of which was Hsi Shih who had been presented by the King of Yüeh. The rhyme-category is *yü*, "beauty," which underscores the theme of Hsi Shih causing the downfall of a nation.

The second poem of this series depicts Cheng Tan, another of Yüeh's Helens, who was sent to Fu Ch'ai along with Hsi Shih:

> Cheng Tan mutely descends the jade staircase,
> Since nightfall arrows have flown, filling the
>   palace door-screens.
> The King of Yüeh must have pointed out the high
>   terrace and laughed—
> Yet I see (only) the gold-engraved lintels of
>   that time.[50]

This verse again describes the King of Yüeh's triumph, apparently somewhat later in the battle sequence. Cheng Tan's silence speaks to the despair of the vanquished. It is too late for words. Words, those with which Wu Tzu-hsü had admonished Fu Ch'ai, warning him of the impending danger of Yüeh, are called to mind by the arrow-filled palace door-screen, for it was before this screen that Wu Tzu-hsü was expected to rethink (the binome for "rethink" is homonymous with "palace door-screen") his arguments before going in to the king. The high terrace in line 3 is of course Ku-su. The King of Yüeh is delighted for he had won two important battles in the shadow of this terrace (see discussion of the first poem in this series immediately above). Line 4 again, as in the preceding poem, contains the poet's evaluation of the king. Here he notes that only the ruins of the once luxuriant palace have stood the test of time. Both the king and the glory of his vengeance were short-lived. This poem is, however, somewhat unorthodox in structure. The parallelism is primarily between couplets rather than contiguous lines. Cheng Tan, her continuous downward movement, and her depression as she ponders the future, are contrasted to the king, his buoyant gesture aloft, and the concern with the past.

The theme of Yüeh's revenge is that of yet another poem on Hsi Shih:

> "Longing for Antiquity at Belle Lodging Palace"
>
> Those voluptuous bones have already turned to
>   fragrant soil,
> The palace wall still presses against the mountain
>   face.

> By crossbow towers rains wash earth away, down to
>   golden arrowheads,
> Along scented paths the mud dissolves revealing jade
>   hairpins.
> Inkwell Pools serve only for the birds from the creek
>   to bathe,
> The slipper staircase is useless, covered by wild
>   flowers.
> The deer at Ku-su truly have nothing to do,
> And should feel regret for that earlier time.[51]

The paradox of bones which are voluptuous sets up a dichotomy of
past and present carried throughout this regulated seven-word-line
poem. The rhyme is again noteworthy: *chia*, "beautiful." Indeed,
the beauty is all of the past. That traces of it which are confined in
soil and mud are still appealing suggests its original grandeur. After
again juxtaposing palace walls and crossbow platforms to the legacy
of the palace women, the third couplet focuses on the present occupants of the baths (line 5) and the stairway made of different
materials for Hsi Shih, so that as she climbed its music would sound
(line 6). The final word in line 5, "to bathe," calls forth visions of Hsi
Shih, but the corresponding word in the line following, "to bury,"
returns the reader to reality. The past has long been buried. Line 7
is pivotal. The deer are a part of the natural ninth-century scene that
the persona overlooks. They are as well symbolic of the licentious
ease of Fu Ch'ai's pleasure palaces.[52] Finally, they fulfill a prophecy
by Wu Tzu-hsü that if more care was not given to Yüeh, the day
would come "when the wild deer would sport over the ruins of the
Ku-su Terrace."[53] But despite the transitionary nature of the deer,
they are incapable of sensing the sadness of the scene, and, like Fu
Ch'ai and Hsi Shih, frolic oblivious to all about them. This concluding couplet is clever in that the persona remains aloof. He never
declares his grief, but only remarks that the deer ought to feel
remorse.

   The most elaborate and refined treatment of this motif, however,
is P'i Jih-hsiu's "Naval Exercise Basin," the eleventh of a series of
twenty verses entitled "Great Lake Poems" written in 870:

> The King of Wu grew weary with ruling his country;
> That with which he amused himself was in the end
>   not enough.

Once he ascended the Ku-su Terrace,
He was still not satisfied with its cramped
   smallness.
5 Dispatch boats clamored through the six palaces.
Floating rams lent awe to the rear guard.
One puff of a deer-musk wind
Ripples in this void the peaceful, clear waters.
Birds endangered shunned the brocade sails,
10 Dragons coiled up in defense against iron axles.
Multicolored streamers excited the misty waves,
Royal standards floated down precipitous gorges.
That spirit-filled region was too much trampled,
Thus they (the spirits) blocked up the Copse House.
15 The vast empyrean was jealous of Great Lake,
Steep roads opened onto the Drilling Ditches.
For several rods chipped stone teeth,
Then a few miles they thread along the sides of
   mountains.
At the bottom it's quiet and looks like gold grease,
20 Broken tiles appear to be grains of cinnabar.
Down at Surf Hall Cheng Tan grows tipsy,
Up in the Toad Pavilion Hsi Shih will spend the
   night.
Several turns on the Misty Mouth Boat,
A single verse of the Arriving Clouds Song.[54]
25 He [Fu Ch'ai] didn't know up on the rail,
That at night the arrowheads of Yüeh would come.[55]
As the Lord King covered his face and died,
His royal concubines didn't dare to weep.
Their voluptuous souls followed waves and whitecaps,
30 As the desolate palaces nourished wild deer.
The country is destroyed, even the sluices grow more
   shallow,
As generations change the grass turns green in vain.
All this the white birds don't know,
Who sleep the morn, then return at dusk to bathe.[56]

Before analyzing this poem, however, let us look at Lu Kuei-meng's
response written in harmony[57] with P'i's verse:

"Naval Exercise Basin"

Yüeh depended on a gentlemanly multitude,[58]
A great general repressed all Wu.[59]

The Wu generals divided the Heavenly Marsh [i.e.,
　　Great Lake] into branches,[60]
To drill ships and instruct troops.
5　One mirror detained in a thousand miles,
The tributaries suddenly meander.
A green cosmetic box binds rolling waves,
Sitting as if in Feng I's body.[61]
Warships one million strong,
10　Floating palaces more than thirty.
Peaceful streams filled with war gongs,
Isolated islands split by barricades.
"Phoenix clubs" cut "cranes' knees" in half,
Brocade yardarms confused among the pennants.
15　Incense smoke and death make up the atmosphere,
Broad and fluid it follows the wind and disperses.
The pellets shot have wiped out the birds on
　　high,
Cups of horn and wood make drunk the fishes in the
　　depths.
The mountain spirits fear being flogged,
20　The watery palace grieves as it becomes a cemetery.
Weapons so sharp they pare the powerful sun,
Yet they were butchered by a rival country.
Down until today spear barbs and arrowheads are left,
Still with the mud and sands intact.
25　Reflected in this moon they cause doubled sorrow,
Coming here the mists seem all the more lonely.
The souls of those brave men still shed tears
Which together have watered green the withering
　　maples.[62]

Again P'i takes us far back into the history of the Great Lake to the
time when it provided the King of Wu, Fu Ch'ai, a training base for
his navies. The poet's field of vision is limited to the luxury and
overindulgence of the king. This is emphasized by the near
paradoxes of a king wearying with his country, for by definition a
king can rule no more than a country. The first line and the next two
probably refer to Fu Ch'ai's decision to try to become the
hegemonist by attacking Ch'i.[63] Ascending Ku-su Terrace would
normally satisfy any monarch, for the view from this pleasure tower
reputedly encompassed an area of over thirty thousand square
miles.[64] Yet Fu Ch'ai desired more. This second couplet is also

disconcerting, for it was after the battle at Ku-su, in which Fu Ch'ai's father Ho Lü was killed, that Fu Ch'ai swore revenge against Yüeh. In P'i's reconstruction, however, we see Fu Ch'ai thinking not merely of Yüeh, but of larger conquests, and not of revenging his father, but of indulging his greed. All else remains enjoyment and play in P'i's poem. Even the armies and navies are only playing at war. They are dangerous, especially in their opulence, so that birds and dragons must take care. There is the miasma of musk winds and other figures which foreshadow doom. The precipitous gorges down which the royal standards marched can be understood metaphorically. Trespassing on the lands of the spirits (the Copse House was a grotto on Western Mountain, an island in Great Lake, where immortals dwelt) and the jealousy of the empyrean had turned even the supernatural against Wu. The steep roads and chipped stone teeth, though part of Wu's opulent, ornamental milieu, are foreboding. This very couplet (lines 17–18) is pivotal. Reading line 20 one realizes that P'i has stepped from the fifth century B.C. down to his present. The steep roads and stone teeth were still there. But the broken tiles suggest the passage of time. The appearance of minerals like gold grease[65] and cinnabar, drugs of immortality, provides a transition, even if not evident except in retrospect, to P'i's illusion of Cheng Tan in a palace beneath the seas and of Hsi Shih ensconced in the moon. At first reading, however, the reader does not notice that these are palaces for immortal women. And this disorients him for a moment. It is into this logical gap that Lu Kuei-meng pours his response. The battles which P'i has transfixed Lu makes his primary concern. He, like any reader of P'i's poem, visualized the training, the battles, and the aftermath of the Wu-Yüeh campaigns. Aside from a few functional allusions needed to set the scene, Lu's verse is a seemingly tangible mental picture of the ditches filled with warships. No more an exercise, this is war! Midst the smoke-filled skies the battle is briefly depicted at its height (lines 11–14):

> Peaceful streams filled with war gongs,
> Isolated islands split by barricades.
> "Phoenix clubs" cut "cranes' knees" in half,
> Brocade yardarms confused among the pennants.

The contrast between the beauties of nature, those of man (even the

weapons are lovely: cranes' knees are a type of spear shaped like the
shinbone of a crane, phoenix clubs are apparently modeled after their
regal namesake)[66], and war's damage to both is best revealed in
these lines. And when the clouds of war completely dissipate (line
16), no scenic landscape is revealed, but a desolate vista in which
the endangered birds (recalling P'i's line 9) have been exterminated
and the dregs of drinking bouts have intoxicated the fish in the
ditches. This couplet (lines 17–18) is very much like the *lien-chü*
(linked verse) technique of expressing the same idea a bit better
than one's partner has done. Lu continues in lines 19 and 20 to twist
images of P'i's poem (cf. P'i's lines 13 and 21). Line 20, although it
may refer to any death, seems to counteract P'i's romantic conception of the demise of Cheng Tan—for Lu she is no immortal, but
rather a corpse. The watery palace is no Shangri-la, but a burial
grounds. In a similar manner to that employed by P'i, Lu moves
from antiquity to his own ninth century A.D. via a part of the physical surroundings which has endured the centuries. But rather than
visualizing the means for everlasting life, Lu sees the implements of
death, spear-barbs and arrowheads, buried in the mud and sand.

In his closing lines P'i depicts the death of Fu Ch'ai and his tears,
the fate of his women, and the fulfillment of Wu Tzu-hsü's prophecy
(see the discussion of "Longing for Antiquity at Belle Lodging
Palace" above). He concludes by echoing the opening couplet of Tu
Fu's "Ch'un-wang" (Spring Prospect) in lines 31 and 32, and by
contrasting nature, whose unsullied creatures, though they resemble, perhaps, Wu's women in loveliness and habit (sleeping late and
bathing at dusk), are truly innocent, to mankind with its greed and
its historical sense of remorse. Lu, as one might expect, does not
react to these lines directly. Their images are stark. The text asks
little of the reader here. So Lu continues in the vein in which he
began, filling in the gap between Wu's greatness and its decline. His
last four lines are centered upon the fate of the men whose lives
were offered to slow the fall of Wu. It is their continuing presence,
as unrequited spirits, that keeps green another of the natural links
with the past, the maple trees.

B. *The flora of Wu*

Another common poetic subject in P'i Jih-hsiu's Soochow corpus
was horticulture. Whether his sinecure allowed him more time
for such traditional pursuits of retirement, or the lush Wu vegeta-

tion attracted him, or his colleagues there interested him in this avocation, P'i seems to have spent hours admiring flowers and recording this admiration in poems such as the following "Song of the Pomegranate":

> The cicada chirps on the autumn branch, locust leaves
>   are yellow,
> The pomegranate fragrance grows old, anxious about
>   chilling frosts.
> Floating clouds embrace the dye, a purple, parrot
>   grain,
> In yellow wax wrappers, in a red-gourd chamber;
> A jade-carved pitcher for ice, containing the
>   moisture of dew,
> Mottled as if it bore tears of the Hsiang Goddesses.
> When a young miss is first married, she has a taste
>   for the sweet and the sour,
> And chews up thousands of crystallike grains.[67]

The first couplet sets the autumnal scene: the pomegranate fruit has lost its deep red blossoms and seen its scent grow old. The fruit itself, however, opens at this time of year revealing hundreds of little crimson seeds, some sweet, some sour. In line 3 P'i begins to describe the pomegranate from the inside out. The dye-centered clouds are the translucent kernels with red-seed centers, which resemble purple parrot grain. The yellow waxlike wrappers refer to the internal sections of the pomegranate, each set off by a waxy, yellowish membrane. The red-gourd chamber is the outer shell of the fruit. The jade pitcher is the skin, blotched as if mottled by the tears of the Hsiang Maidens. "A young miss" attempts to render *hsiao-niang*, a general term for young girls during the T'ang (young men were called *hsiao-lang*). There is as well a matrix of allusions and borrowings which suggest the poem may have been written as an epithalamium.[68] Line 5 reflects Wang Ch'ang-ling's (698–ca. 765) "Fu-jung lou sung Hsin Chien" [Seeing Off Hsin Chien at the Hibiscus Tower]: "If Loyang friends or relatives ask about me,/ [Say] an icy heart in a jade pitcher."[69] The gist of this couplet is that although not able to return with Hsin Chien to the capital, Wang's heart remains pure and faithful. The following line refers to the wives of Shun who drowned and became the deities of the Hsiang River. They, too, suggest fidelity, since their tears are spent longing

for their dead husband. They are also, however, the object of sha-
man suitors in the *Songs of the South*,[70] preparing the seventh line
and its reference to the sweet-sour first days of a marriage. The
pomegranate is the apt subject of a poem on marriage, as it was a
common gift at weddings, because of its many seeds and the fertility
they symbolize (*tzu*, "seeds," is a homonym for "children"). The
abundance of words suggesting marriage or sensualness ("embrace,"
"red . . . chamber," "candle," "jade," "have a taste for") enhance
the possibility of this reading.

Often, however, P'i wrote of flowers not as symbolic of an event,
but purely as aesthetic objects:

> "Moved to Record My Feelings by the Full Flowering
> of the Dwarf Pomegranate Blossoms
> in My Courtyard—Written While Ill"
>
> In a single night springtime split the crimson sacks,
> On the branches an oily green resplendent in the
> daylight.
> When the winds are smooth they just seem to be changed
> into red dew,
> I only worry that they'll become a vermilion frost in
> the warmth of the sun.
> Purple jade fills the branches to roast the night moon,
> Gold elixirs enclose the pistils to drop on the morning
> sun.
> I don't know if the cassia tree understands emotion,
> And stays Lord Lu from amusing himself endlessly with me.[71]

This poem is another example of P'i's predilection for shades of
red.[72] The first four lines are striking: a springtime night and the
following morning are the backdrop for crimson buds just opened,
their lubricious leaves of green, and the similes of the blossoms as
red dew and vermilion frost; all these metaphoric visions are
perhaps a result of P'i's illness. This scene is followed by the picture
of the jade-blossoms (literally "flames of equal height") of the night
and their dew in the dawn (golden elixir) administering to sun and
moon. From the persona's limited point of view the blossoms may
seem to near the moon, and certainly the morning sun must emerge
beneath the branches so that it might receive the ablutions of the
pistils; but this is the height of the diseased perception created by

the first six lines. This feverish introduction lends the final couplet a particular subtlety. The cassia tree is a refined plant, with fragile blossoms, a delicate fragrance, and no fruit. This image of purity introduces the addressee, Lu Kuei-meng (Lord Lu), and praises his refined and perhaps somewhat aloof nature—unsure of whether the fiery exultations of lines 1–6 are comprehensible to him.[73]

The following poem involves Lu Kuei-meng once again:

> "Early Spring, Sending Oranges to Lu-wang"
>
> One by one with branch and leaves I offer this
>   freshness,
> So bright in color it seems the mists of Lake
>   Tung-t'ing are still on their skins.
> They aren't the heavy golden pellets of Han
>   Yen,
> They're just the round jade treasures of the
>   King of Chou.
> Cut open—the sun's essence just broken open,
> Tossed about—the marrow of a meteor before it
>   vanishes.
> I know you've often been ill, but you'll still
>   "obtain sagehood,"
> So I've sent all these cold buds to your bedside.[74]

This poem apparently accompanied a branch of an orange tree, replete with its fruit, sent as a gift. The branch, of course, served to testify to the freshness of the fruit, for if it had been picked for some time, the leaves would have withered. The allusions to Han Yen and King Mu of Chou underline the strong feelings growing between P'i and Lu: Han Yen was a favorite of Emperor Wu of the Han who was given golden pellets to shoot as a means of passing time,[75] while King Mu received a jade treasure from the Hsi-wang-mu during his brief tête-à-tête with that famous goddess.[76] After the introductory first couplet and the development of the description of the oranges in allusive metaphors, the third couplet raises the imagery skyward. The final two lines play upon two idioms: "sagehood" refers to the best-quality clear wines (as opposed to "worthiness"—turbid, lower quality wines); "cold buds," which might serve as a literal metaphor for the oranges, indicates any sort of an unrefined gift. Some knowledge of traditional pharmacology will further lend a unity to the poem, for the white, pulpy threads enclosing the flesh of the orange

were used to stop thirst and vomiting after drinking, and cakes made
from oranges were employed as a means of sobering up.[77]

The following *chüeh-chü*, "Again on the Rose," is also steeped in
vibrant reds:

> Thick like an orangutan's blood smeared on a
>   white cloth,
> Light as the swallows intending to fly to the top
>   of the sky—
> What a pity this delicate beauty can scarcely
>   stand the sun:
> It throws its rays upon the deep reds, creating
>   lighter reds.[78]

This little verse is based upon three techniques common to P'i's
Soochow corpus: an attention to color, use of simile, and the ap-
propriation of phrases from a predecessor. The similes of the first
two lines (A.C. Graham has argued that increased use of the simile
was one characteristic of late T'ang poetry[79]) serve as a comment on
the title-topic. They describe the appearance of the rose in terms of
its color (resembling blood), its weight (light as swallows), and its
texture (like cloth). However, in the final lines the rose is seen, as in
so much of late T'ang poetic matter, as something which appears
more beautiful indoors or in a secluded garden. The final line is a
variation of Tu Fu's "Which are more delightful, the dark red or the
light?"[80]

P'i's interest in the lovely women of Wu has already been demonstrated. Thus, since flowers are commonly a symbol for women, it
should come as no surprise that mildly erotic elements would enter
into these descriptions, as in the following "In Yang-chou Viewing
Magnolia Blossoms":

> They crush the fragrant clump of one thousand
>   blooms which precede the twelfth lunar month,
> So sheer and smooth they unexpectedly surpass the
>   white crab apple's merits.
> A cicada's head silent, mantled in the morning
>   snow,
> The musk deer's scent bag ownerless, serves the spring wind.

> If one branch sweeps the ground, a Jasper Garden
>   is formed,
> With several trees high and low in the courtyard
>   we've a Flowery Palace.
> I presume it must have been the clothing of the
>   Heavenly Daughters in the past,
> For until now it still hasn't released its full
>   red.[81]

This *hsin-i (Magnolia kobus)* tree grows to a height of seventy-five feet and produces large (four inches across) white flowers with tiny spots of red in late winter (early spring on the lunar calendar of P'i's day) before its leaves have opened. Since Yang-chou is a city known for beautiful women, and since women are so often associated with flowers, it is only appropriate that much of the imagery of this poem could be equally applied to a woman.

The first couplet aligns the *hsin-i* and its competition—the other flowers which bloom in the following months. The rhyme-category, *tung* "east" is appropriate symbolically and temporally (as the correlating direction for spring and love in the paradigm of the five elements). The fourth word in line 1, *ya (QA*)*, is striking in the original. Its polysemous range of meanings—secondary, to render second or inferior, ugly, or to make ugly, and finally to press or weigh down—all suggest the superiority and priority (as a first-month flower) of the *hsin-i* blossoms. It also fits well into the sound pattern of this couplet, dominated by alliterative and rhyming (or near-rhyming) compounds (reconstructed pronunciation is after Hugh Stimson's *The Jongyuan In Yunn;*[82] even-tone syllables are in lower case, uneven in capitals): *"LAP tshen tshen TUA QA phiang tshing,/ SEI NIH phien sieng SUɨ NA king."* In the second line *SEI* and *NHɨ* (sheer and smooth) are both terms often associated with a woman. But the sense of this line is to emphasize that the *hsin-i* is not to be praised only for its uniquely early appearance, but that it can as well hold its own vis-à-vis other first month blossoms like the crab apple.

In the second couplet the comparison to a woman, somewhat adumbrated in line 2, is given clear expression. "Cicada's head" alludes to poem fifty-seven, "Shih jen" (The Stately Lady), in the *Book of Poetry*, where one finds a catalog of a woman's beauty similar to the "Songs of Solomon":

Her hands are like soft young shoots, her skin is
    like lard;
Her neck is like the tree-grub, her teeth are like
    melon-seeds,
Her head is cicada-like, her eyebrows are silk-
    worm-like;
Her artfully smiling (mouth) is red, her
    beautiful eyes are well-defined black and
    white.[83]

Yet this "cicada's head" cannot speak and is quilted with the tran-
sient snow (this snow may as well be metaphoric—snow in Yang-
chou in February is not common) of an early morning. The sensual
fragrance of the *hsin-i* is then likened to that of the musk deer. Yet
this scent is innocent, with no master, and submits only to the
spring breezes.

The third couplet develops the metaphoric portrayal further. As a
branch is bent to the earth by these breezes, its beauty seems to
transform the grove into the Jasper Garden, the home of the goddess Hsi-wang-mu on Mount K'un-lun. The uneven silhouettes of
trees of various height seem as if they are the towers and pavilions of
the Flowery Palace, a heavenly residence known for its botanical
beauties.

The final couplet continues this image, as the heavenly daughters
must inhabit this palace.[84] Since their garments were no doubt pure
white, the red spots on the *hsin-i* blossoms have, in the poet's
opinion, not yet been able to develop completely. The ambivalent
yet naively sensual depiction of these blossoms tightens the relationship between feminine and floral imagery and lends a mildly
erotic tone to this poem.

The final floral poem to be examined, "Elecampane Blossoms,"
illustrates yet another approach to the flowers of Soochow:

Yin and *yang* were the charcoal, earth the kiln,
Smelting brought forth golden coins without using
    a mold.
Don't turn a relaxed and satisfied face toward
    people,
For it's hard to tell if you bring relief to the
    poor and needy.[85]

The yellow blossoms of the elecampane were introduced from abroad during the sixth century through Canton. There girls sold them strung, as T'ang coins were, on multicolored thread.[86] Playing on the comparison between the flower and a coin, the blossoms are first depicted in numismatic terms. The final couplet at first reading seems merely a witty closing. But "turn a satisfied face" is an allusion to the *Analects:* "On entering the palace he [the gentleman] seems to shrink into himself . . . on coming [from an audience], after descending the first step *his expression relaxed into one of satisfaction and relief* " [italics mine].[87] Thus, there seems to be a veiled criticism of officialdom (or a self-criticism, cf. "Three Poems of Shame" above) in these lines. Though the "gold-coin flowers" in name would seem to be of value to the poverty stricken, actually they are not. Similarly, those officials emerging from an imperial audience should have spoken on behalf of the needy, as befits their duty, but actually they (or P'i himself) did not.

C. *Reclusion*

Another category of P'i's later poetry was reclusion. He had approached it philosophically, considering its merits as a possible lifestyle, while at Deer-Gate. In Soochow, however, he ostensibly presents descriptive accounts of actual hermits, such as his "Poems of Two Journeys" (only the preface and the second of these works is presented here):

Among the gentry of the Wu Region is the [former] Administrator of Enwang Palace,[88] Hsü Hsiu-chü, who maintained a library of over ten thousand volumes which had been handed down to him. He was at ease and content with himself. I borrowed several thousand volumes of his books. In less than a year I completely fulfilled an earlier ambition, drinking deeply, surfeiting myself in classic and history, sometimes forgetting to eat or drink until late in the day. And then there is the previous Chief of Employees at Ching County, Jen Hui. The place where he lives has deep groves and winding pools, lofty pavilions and quiet stone staircases. I also went there to see him. Sometimes when I had free time after my official duties, I'd go there to relax. The hermitic affairs of glade and fount we would put into verse with no hesitation. At least every ten days I visit these two residences. Therefore, I made songs to leave behind, named them the "Two Journeys," and sent them as well to Lu Lu-wang [Lu Kuei-meng].

"Mr. Jen"

Mr. Jen indulges himself, lofty and unrestrained;
Few can attain his way of doing things.
In a house leisurely placed by a wood and spring,
His whole life he's kept away from the clamor of the world.
5 I understand he once served the people,
But his "good-for-nothing" nature made him incapable of
    holding office.
Abruptly he untied his sash with the official seal,
Leaving it as one does an old shoe,
And came back to his home village,
10 To be united with friends and relatives.
In diverting the stream he worked like a hardy young man,
After the buildings were all arranged he acknowledged
    his good work.
For one hundred paces after entering the gate,
The wind rustles through ancient trees.
15 Broad railings lean out on a small hill,
Contoured verandas enclose unusual rocks.
White lotus droop on the balustrades,
Verdant birds move along the curtain ledges.
The lay of the land resembles Five Drains,
20 Shapes of hillsides are like those in the Three Gorges.
Gibbons sleep, fat and soft,
Wild ducks feed, quacking now and then.
He parts the floating heart to drop a fishing line,
Knots wisteria to tie the cassia-wood oars.
25 He detains the itinerant tree-doctor at the gate,
Leans his flower-planting trowel against the wall.
Passing the years in rough cotton clothes,
From day to day wearing his white kerchief.
Even as he closed his door to many people,
30 He looked upon me as someone especially welcome.
He asked me to inscribe his roof beam,
Kept me sitting on the stone couch.
My soul sauntered with the pure scenery,
Mists and fog I let permeate my clothes.
35 He allowed the tortoise to ascend his stairs,
The gulls approach him on his bed.
His pools are like glossy mirrors,
In which one sees fish blink.
His cups are ladles all made from fir knots,
40 His platters are utensils only of lotus leaves.

Leisurely drinking, not handing each other "fines."
Leisurely playing at chess, without trying too hard.
A leisurely day, one need not set his hat straight,
Leisurely breezes, why bother with a fan?
45 With such a place to contemplate,
How could I tire of following my Way?
In robes of high officials one competes to outshine
    the other,
Midst drums and pipes one struggles to drown
    the other out.
Those who have desires understand how to push to
    the front,
50 Those who slander are good at whispering in one's ear.
Power and influence can be lost in an instant,
And punishment and misfortune pile one upon the other.
At this time I'll not admit this little hole
To be inferior to the rich Gates of Heaven.
55 Here there is a home where one can rest,
Books in which one can fish and hunt.
I want to stay with Mr. Jen
And be content with this until my dying day.[89]

In the brief introduction to this section above it was noted that P'i ostensibly portrayed actual recluses. But this long poem depicts perhaps as much P'i's conception of an ideal man who has retired from society as it does Jen Hui. Despite the many details which seem to describe Jen, the entire poem could be applied, with few alterations, to any recluse. This verse, often cited as an example of Han Yü's influence on P'i,[90] follows a single rhyme-category: *ho*, "harmony." Thus it is best divided by content alone. Following the long description of Jen's life and his retreat (lines 1–32), P'i turns to his own reaction, a mental journey of sorts, to Jen Hui's estate. Beginning with line 41, emphasis upon a life devoid of all forms of competition is outlined. This is then followed by a more political application of these principles (lines 47–52). In between (line 46), P'i makes it clear that his "Way," at least at the time this poem was composed, was at one with that of Jen Hui. And yet in the final couplet P'i implies that although it is his desire to stay with Jen, he is unable to. For he is a man who, though thwarted in his attempts to "push to the front," has not yet the reclusive purity to attract the skittish gulls to his bedside.

The theme of de-emphasizing competition is supported by the

idea of being in harmony with nature and man. The examples of the former are evident. And even though Jen is a recluse, his long chats with the tree-doctor and with P'i, and his leisurely life (the Chinese term *hsien* has only positive associations and connotes a life of purity and simplicity), illustrate his harmonious relations with some men at least.

Aside from these verses on Jen and Hsü, P'i also wrote a series of ten verses on another typical Chinese recluse, the woodcutter. The sixth of this series, "A Woodcutter's Ax," illustrates a tone which throughout differs greatly from "Two Journeys":

> With a large ax handle tucked at his waist,
> Straight on and deep into the ravine he goes.
> At the sound of a single blow in the empty grove,
> Hidden birds call one another to flight.
> Trees felled, tigers are driven off;
> Nests overturned, forest goblins wail.
> I don't know of anyone who wields the big ax
> Who can do away with evils like this![91]

This poem is included in Teng T'o's modern [1958] version of the *T'ang shih san-pai shou* (Three Hundred Poems of the T'ang).[92] Although prosodically it typifies this series, there is one added dimension which may have appealed particularly to People's Republic critics. That is the political connotation of the poem. The fifth line reads literally: "Felling trees drives off 'Father Li'." "Father Li" is of course a euphemism for the tiger, but it might also be an indirect reference to the T'ang emperors, also surnamed Li. The seventh line has an even clearer political significance. "The big ax" was an imperial token which permitted the recipient to execute evildoers on his own. Reading in retrospect topical allegorical references to the fall of the T'ang at the hands of such simple men as this idealized woodcutter is more than a little risky. But there is a political level to this poem not found in most of the series.

"Woodcutters' Families," the second of these ten poems, is, for example, a direct portrayal of the rustic life of these men of the forests:

> In some deepest spot in the vast mountains,
> Two or three families have lived since antiquity.
> They have shared former eras with clouds and creepers,

Earned their livelihood alongside apes and birds,
Cleansed their clothes in vernal springs,
Cooked their meals from wild flowers.
Living here one old man after another,
Not a one understanding the sorrows of old age.[93]

Although in translation, because of its eight-line structure and semantic parallelism, this poem may seem to be a new-style verse, it is actually an old-style five-word-line composition. In fact, P'i seems to have given the aural effect little attention, for the fourth line is made up entirely of level-tone syllables[94] and would no doubt have made a strange impression when read aloud by a ninth-century reader. The simple diction and rather relaxed syntactical system are more in keeping with an old-style poem and with the subject itself. Nevertheless, the couplets do tend to close off into units and to function much as they would in a new-style poem: the subject is presented in the first two lines, described in terms of its environs in the second and third couplets, and commented upon in the final two lines. Such poems as this mark one sort of reaction to the overemphasis on prosody in the new-style poetry of the early ninth century. It provides, moreover, an apt transition to P'i's prosodic experiments.

D. *Miscellaneous poetry*

There are a number of poetic games or experiments which have become accepted subgenres in the Chinese poetic tradition. This type of poetry is often termed *tsa-t'i shih* (poetry of miscellaneous forms) and includes forms such as the *li-ho* (splitting and rejoining characters), *hui-wen* (palindromes), *chi-chü* (combining [extant] lines), *tsa-sheng-yün* (poems in which one or two initials, finals, or tones are used throughout), and *feng-jen* (a form based on paronomasia).[95] P'i was not only one of the earliest poets to explore so many of these forms, he also believed that poetry was evolving in this direction. He recognized that poetry developed in close connection with music. And since he had undoubtedly noted the changes in T'ang music, he concluded that "miscellaneous-form poetry" (and not the *tz'u* lyrics with which he was also familiar) would eventually supplant new-style poetry: "Alas, from ancient to regulated, from regulated to miscellaneous, the way of poetry is thus exhausted therein!"[96] Thus, these poems, which are at best

interesting experiments for a modern reader, were those which P'i
hoped would herald a new age of poetry.

In all P'i wrote forty such poems, including the following "Palin-
drome on Rising at Dawn Presented to Harmonize with Lu Lu-
wang [Kuei-meng]":

> Lonely smoke rises in the morning, curving across the
>   early plain,
> Scattered trees faintly divided, cut in half by the waves;
> Back of the lake the fishing pole was moved by the
>   night rain,
> Next to my headrest the bamboo is blown awry by the winds.
> The plum in the painting bears a sheen as if the ink were still
>   slightly moist,
> The lichen in the picture has been steamed and lost half its red.[97]
> With nothing to do a wine cup lasts the entire day,
> Together with you I'd just like to hide beyond the
>   eastern wall.[98]

The poem is a seven-word regulated poem. It is not a particularly
interesting piece, but technically does fit the prosodic patterns and
rhyme-scheme even when read backwards, for the tonal-scheme of
the last four lines is a mirror image of the first quatrain.[99] When
read in reverse the poem yields the following:

> Hermitic pleasures of the eastern wall, I only share with you,
> All day long I hold a wine cup, asking if there's anything to do.
> The red is lost as if it were half steamed after painting the lichen,
> Black ink moist lightly shines in a picture of plums.
> The winds in the morning blow against my headrest, as I
>   sleep alongside the bamboo.
> The rainy night shifted the pole, fishing in the lake out back;
> The waves in the middle divide in half, faint trees seem to scatter;
> Above the curving plain a whisp of morning smoke rises early.

The syntax and sense of this reverse reading is particularly loose.
The translator and reader are thrown back upon poetic conventions
to make sense of these lines. Such poems are certainly those which
inspired Hu Chen-heng's criticism that P'i's weakness was "putting
his brush to paper so that words preceded feeling and there was
neither wind nor bone to act as a frame." Yet in a sense they are of
interest to modern structuralist critics, for both they and P'i Jih-

hsiu, in these works at least, are primarily concerned with language and its structural possibilities.

P'i also wrote *tsa-sheng-yün*, such as the following "In A Bitter Rain Again Writing Four-tone Poems to Send to Lu-wang, Four Poems, Number Four: Level and Entering Tones":

> Put up midst a never-ending rain,
> In a ramshackle hut under a rough roof beam,
> Lotus leaves droop—and frighten the fish,
> Bamboo branches drip—raindrops hitting the crane.
> An idle monk strums a thousand-sound zither,
> A guest in lodging has only a sachel of herbs.
> Distant, my thoughts are of you when
> Suddenly I remember to put on my waxed clogs.[100]

In this five-word regulated poem the first couplet introduces the scene and the situation. The second and third, which are lines of some poetic merit, amplify the scene. The "guest" in line 6 is probably the poet himself. This prepares the final expression in the fourth couplet of the poet lost in reverie of his friend. But the tonal pattern follows no regulated scheme. The first line of each couplet is made up only of even-tone words, the second contains solely uneven-tone syllables:

> KJE SEI TSHHULHMTHNG, kheut thaek qik mik qak;
> HA KHIUENG HUAN KIAENG NGH, tiik tek phiik
>   tsiuik hak;
> HEN SENG TSHEN SIENG KHJHM, siik khaek qiit khiep iak.
> HU NIEN SIE PHIUI KIUEN, huet qiek lap kniek thiak.

The result is a bifurcation between smooth level and cacophonic lines which not only reinforces the sense (especially in lines 2, 4, and 8 where the final consonants are particularly apt in suggesting rain dripping or the slap of wooden clogs), but also adds a new dimension to the structure of the poem by strengthening the textural associations between lines which have the same tone (i.e., one-three-five-seven and two-four-six-eight). In other words, the fourth word SIENG*, "sound," of line 5, which normally is read in the context of its own line, TSHEN SIENG KHJHM, "thousand-sound zither," and its foil in the same couplet, qiit khiep iak, "one bag of herbs," is now as well understood as a partner to the even-numbered level-tone lines, and especially to the fourth word in these lines. LI⧸M*, "never-ending rain," in line 1 and KIAENG*, "to frighten," from line 3 share strong textural ties with SIENG*. The overall impression of this poem would seem to lead the reader, after a perusal of the semantic content, to the linguistic possibilities of this "structure."

"An Alliterative Poem Entitled 'Thoughts Brookside' " is similar:

> Sparse pines hang their heads through to the shore,
> A cold crane comes down crashing across waves.
> The bright colors of the brush seem to linger,
> The shape of the clouds is vacantly placid and
>   peaceful.[101]

Translation of the final two lines is difficult. The idea of line 3 is that the vegetation is hesitating to reveal its brightest colors (as a threatening sky seems to hesitate before it rains). Line 4 is problematic because of the third syllable, khing*, which holds "empty," "in the sky," "in vain" among its meanings and which parallels as well iuik*, "on the point of," in line 3. But again the merits of this poem lie in its sound patterns: "SI⧸ SHAEM TEI TH⧸NG THAN, laeng lu⧸ li⧸p luan lang;/ tsau tshei iu⧸k I⧸I I⧸U, HIUEN IU⧸NG khing tham thang." The first couplet is a particular instance of harmonizing sound with sense, as the pines gently lean through the level tones of the first line, followed by the five alliterative, deflected-tone syllables which herald the lu⧸'s (actually a type of egret) landing on the brook.

Finally, one should examine one of the *lien-chü* (linked-line) poems that P'i and his colleagues wrote. The following "Linked-line Verse Written at a Literary Party on the Night Before the Cold Food Festival" was written by P'i, Lu Kuei-meng, and Chang Pen,[102] a fellow poet and a member of the Soochow literary coterie in the early 870s:

> The literary stars are gathered tonight.
> They should be between the Dipper and the Ox. [P'i]
> The man who carried the stone has just arrived,
> The traveler who went by raft is not yet back. [Chang]
> Passing around the cups to "luxuriant dew songs,"
> Eliciting lines from those cloudy-white countenances. [Lu]
> For tempo and cadence, just listen to the bamboo,

In idle chats only speak of mountains. [P'i]
When in discussion one is stumped, he pours forth
   his "imperial collection,"
10 When they argue furiously they break open the
   Buddhist collection. [Chang]
When wines of Ling are divided, everyone has a
   share of the green,
If paper from Pa breaks open, it shows its redness. [Lu]
Listening to pure talk sobers one up,
Forcing rhymes are difficult to fit in. [P'i]
15 Take the rhinoceros-horn ladle, face the wind and bow,
Toy with the amber jade branch, gazing toward the
   moon. [Chang]
Just as the pines sough,
I recall in a dream of a fountain the trickling
   sounds of a shallow stream. [Lu]
Our literary drafts from one of these gatherings
Couldn't be thrown out by Chao-ming himself! [P'i][103]

These twenty lines contain more than their share of enigmatic
phrases. P'i's first couplet plays on "literary stars," which is both a
heavenly configuration (located between the Chinese constellations
the South Dipper [Sagittarius] and the Ox [Capricorn]), and a
eulogistic metaphor for P'i and his two companions. The second
couplet, by Chang Pen, links heaven and earth. "The traveler who
went by raft" alludes to a story in Chang Hua's (232–300) *Po wu
chih*[104] about a man who sailed from his island home to the place
where the Milky Way and the sea meet. He sailed on and saw the
weaving girl and the herd boy, occupants of the heavens. Then he
returned home to find that he had appeared as a "stranger star" in
the constellation of the Ox (where the herd boy lives). The allusion
in line 3 is more obscure, but seems to refer to a narrative from the
Chi-lin[105] in which another man visited the source of the Milky
Way. He met a woman there washing silk gauze (the weaving girl)
and carried home a stone she gave him. The stone turned out to be
that which had propped up the loom of the weaving girl. In this line
it would seem that this "man" is actually referring to a star which has
just come out. Similarly, the "stranger star," probably a nova, has
not reappeared for this gathering. Both allusions may also, however,
have some more literal and personal significance among this group
of poets. Lu Kuei-meng's third couplet is nearly unintelligible be-

cause the luxuriant-dew songs and the cloudy countenances remain
unidentified. The next four lines, by P'i and Chang, render advice to
the conversationalist (and perhaps to the poet), P'i urging a natural
line and Chang extolling the value of reference works. Lu then
turns, in the sixth couplet, to the accoutrements of the poem, wine
and paper. The seventh verse speaks of the poet at his craft and is
followed by lines in which wine, nature, and the moon are cultivated as sources of inspiration.[106] The penultimate ninth couplet, by
Lu Kuei-meng, suggests that poetry is no more than the sounds of
nature. Given this incongruous eighteen-line prelude, P'i can do
little else in closing than to praise the poetry of these gatherings,
perhaps with tongue in cheek. As a series of personal images and
references, with little larger structure than the tenuous theme of
poetic inspiration and creation, the poem tends to break into couplets.

IV *Concluding Remarks*

Having examined selections from the most important divisions of
P'i Jih-hsiu's verse, one can see that P'i is a very representative late
T'ang poet. The unfolding of his poetics encompasses both of the
major schools of this era. His concerns run the gamut of possible
subjects, from starving peasants to metaphoric comparisons of himself to a star. The direction of his literary development, however,
from the didacticism of his old-style verse through the aesthetic and
technical concerns of his regulated-verse efforts, carefully parallels
his psychological state. Although preparing for the examinations
certainly compounded his early fervor, it is basically P'i's identification with the peasantry which is noteworthy in his earliest work.
When he failed to find a place in the bureaucracy of the capital city,
he turned, disillusioned, to the very patterned and personal new-
style verse. Although there is some degree of didacticism in this
later work, it is directed to an increasingly smaller audience, and
thereby neglects his previous convictions that literature was a social
force. In many ways P'i's early songs of social and political import
became, in his later years, requests for his own well-being.

CHAPTER 5

Evaluation: An Envoi

I *Introduction*

THE significance of a literatus like P'i Jih-hsiu is twofold. Firstly, as a man who drastically changed his approach to life and literature in his middle years, he has left a corpus which has been many things to many people. His earlier work has often elicited praise from didactic critics; the Soochow corpus appeals more to students of the exotic or those interested in linguistic experiments in literature. By tracing the reception of these works one can learn much of literary taste and its evolution. Secondly, the relationship between the evolution of P'i's psychological state and that of his literary style is another subject which should interest many contemporary literary critics. But this second subject has already been explored above. In this concluding chapter one should hope, therefore, to trace P'i's literary posterity, to assess his current status, and to project as much as possible the trend of future evaluations of his work.

II *History of the Traditional Reception of P'i's Works*

The earliest record (aside from P'i's own prefaces) of P'i Jih-hsiu's writings is to be found in the *Pei-meng so-yen* [Odds and Ends from the Northern Part of Meng Marsh] by Sun Kuang-hsien (d. 968). There the *Wen-sou* and *P'i tzu* [Master P'i, i.e., *Lu-men yin-shu*] are noted.[1] The "Bibliographic Treatise" in the *Hsin T'ang shu* (New T'ang History)[2] adds a *Hsü-t'ai chi* [Collection from Hsü Pavilion (Hsü Pavilion is another name for Ku-su Terrace in Soochow)] which seems to have been a separate collection of P'i's Soochow writings (no longer extant). There is some indication that a great number of P'i's writings have been lost.[3] Indeed, the reputation of P'i's connections with Huang Ch'ao seems to have affected his literary fortune

for some time. None of his works is included in the nearly coeval
Ts'ai-tiao chi [Collection of Verses by Talented Men] compiled by
Wei Hu (fl. 910) which does collect poems by such contemporary
and kindred minds as Lu Kuei-meng (five poems), Lai Ku (d. 881;
two verses), Lo Yin (seventeen), and Tu Hsün-ho (eight).

P'i's popularity increased markedly during the Sung dynasty. His
prose (thirteen pieces) and poetry (six selections) is well represented
in the eleventh-century anthology, *T'ang-wen sui* [Fragments of
T'ang Prose] compiled by Yao Hsüan (968–1020) in reaction to the
tone of the *Wen-yüan ying-hua*. Wang An-shih (1021–1086) included six of P'i's poems in his *T'ang pai-chia shih-hsüan* [Selected
Verse of One hundred T'ang Poets].[4] These selections are almost
totally from the *Wen-sou*. This is in part attributable to the didactic
tastes of the compilers, but also seems to be related to the availabil-
ity of P'i's respective collections. The *Wen-sou,* circulated in the
capital as a means of obtaining a reputation prior to P'i's examination
success, was much more widely known than the Soochow poems.
Indeed, the *Wen-sou* is cited by such Sung bibliophiles as Ch'ao
Kung-wu (d. 1171),[5] Ch'en Chen-sun (*ca.* 1190–1249),[6] and Hung
Mai (1123–1202).[7] During the Yüan dynasty Hsin Wen-fang (fl.
1304) praised P'i's didactic pieces and condemned his later work in
his *T'ang ts'ai-tzu chuan*[8] notice of P'i. With the Ming dynasty,
interest in all aspects of P'i's writings grew—the *Wen-sou* was
printed twice during the early part of the sixteenth century,[9] a
separate collection of P'i's works written in Soochow appeared during the Wan-li period (1575–1619),[10] and several prose essays were
collected in the *Shuo-fu.*[11] Although over four hundred of P'i's
poems were gathered to be included in the *Ch'üan T'ang-shih*
(Complete Poetry of the T'ang) by Ts'ao Yin (1658–1712) and his staff
in the first decade of the eighteenth century, the Ch'ing dynasty
anthology, *T'ang-shih san-pai shou*, which has had much to do with
shaping the literary taste of subsequent generations, represented
late T'ang poetry through the poems of Li Shang-yin (twenty-four
poems), Tu Mu (ten), and Wen T'ing-yün (four), all members of the
"aesthetic school."

III *Modern Reassessments of P'i Jih-hsiu*

Thus by the early part of this century P'i's reputation had reached
a nadir. Yet the variety of his corpus began to rescue him. Lu Hsün
[Chou Shu-jen] (1881–1936), noting the similarity between the

satirical vignettes of P'i and Lu Kuei-meng and those of his generation, praised P'i's essays.[12] Moreover, several anthologies of the
early May Fourth Period included P'i's poems,[13] and numerous
early historians of Chinese literature, such as Ku Shih, Hu Yün-i,
and T'an Cheng-pi, all mention P'i.[14] The 1930s saw P'i's critical
theories discussed by Kuo Shao-yü in his *Chung-kuo wen-hsüeh
p'i-p'ing-shih* [History of Chinese Literary Criticism] (1934) as one
of the final echoes of the T'ang neoclassical movement.[15] Nearly a
decade later, Wen I-to included nine of P'i's poems in his "T'ang-
shih ta-hsi" [Outline of T'ang Poetry].[16]

Since the mid-fifties interest in P'i and his corpus has grown
steadily. He is mentioned in most histories of literature, of poetry,
and of literary criticism. Numerous critical articles have appeared
discussing his life and works and three were included in the collection *T'ang-shih yen-chiu lun-wen chi* [A Collection of Essays Inves-
tigating T'ang Poetry] (1959).[17] Nearly five thousand copies of his
Literary Marsh, newly collated, edited, and punctuated by Hsiao
Ti-fei, were printed by Chung-hua shu-chü by 1965.[18] Finally,
seven of his poems were included in Teng To's *Hsin-pien T'ang-shih
san-pai-shou*.[19] And given the present regard for Lu Hsün in the
People's Republic of China, one can expect that P'i will continue to
receive both praise and critical attention. Most recently, two of his
essays were included in a revised version of Chang Ch'i-wen's
T'ang-tai san-wen hsüan chu [Annotated Selections of Prose Writings from the T'ang Period] (Peking: Chung-hua shu-chü, 1977).
And finally, the second volume of Liu Ta-chieh's recent revision of
his history of Chinese literature devotes an entire section to him:
"P'i Jih-hsiu and Other [Late T'ang] Authors."[20] Liu divides the
poetry of the late ninth century into two subdivisions: 1) that of large
landowners, such as Han Wo (844–923) and Ssu-k'ung T'u (837–
908), who feared the imminent class struggle of the late T'ang and
tended to withdraw from society, and 2) that of poor scholars and
ill-starred officials (often one condition dictated the other) who presented the social struggle of the times in their works. P'i is also seen
as legalist-inclined, and the preface to his music bureau poetry is
traced to Po Chü-i's "Hsin yüeh-fu hsü" [Preface to New Music
Bureau Poetry].[21]

In the West critical recognition of P'i's works came first in the
writings of Edward Schafer. In *The Vermilion Bird* and *Golden
Peaches of Samarkand*, P'i's poetry, especially those luxuriant verses

of his Soochow corpus, is quoted or translated often.[22] Possibly because of the close attention European scholars have paid to publications from the People's Republic, P'i merited a long paragraph by Donald Holzman in *East Asia,* volume one of the *Dictionary of Oriental Literatures,* edited by Jaroslav Prusek and Zbigniew Slupski (London: Allen and Unwin, 1974), pp. 140–141. Several translations of P'i's poetry were included in the most recent anthology of Chinese poetry, *Sunflower Splendor* (Bloomington: Indiana University Press, 1975), edited by Wu-chi Liu and Irving Yucheng Lo.[23] And finally, it is hoped that the present volume will stimulate interest in P'i Jih-hsiu.

IV *Conclusion*

Ts'ao P'i once defined a great writer as a man who mastered all genres. And René Wellek has observed that "minor works (good in the style of the period . . .) gain in reputation when the literature of the day bears some kind of sympathetic relations to that of their day, lose when that relation is adverse."[24] Although P'i is by no means a great writer, he is an important and interesting one, in part because of his attempt to master all genres. The radical transformation of his work late in life, moreover, has assured him a more consistent reputation than Wellek's remarks would lead one to believe, for some aspect of his verse always seems to "bear some kind of sympathetic relations" to contemporary poetry, whatever the fashion may be.

His poetry marks clearly the two major tendencies of the late T'ang and illustrates, perhaps by its inadequacies, some of the reasons which allowed the new *tz'u* lyrics such a prominent place in Sung literature. As an adherent of neoclassical prose, a follower of Han Yü, and an advocate of *Mencius,* P'i is also a forerunner of the Neo-Confucians in both thought and style. His literary experiments, however, although of little interest as poems, may prove as he intended to be of most significance to the future generations. Further examination of their technique and the correspondences with Lu Kuei-meng's similar pieces may reveal a great deal about late T'ang poetics. And finally, owing to his varied corpus, the history of P'i Jih-hsiu's reception and evaluation is of interest to the literary historiographer. He lived in a period of transition toward the end of a millennium of uninterrupted tradition. But he pointed toward the targets of "modern China" which began in Sung society. It would seem, therefore, that although interest in P'i Jih-hsiu's works may vary from generation to generation, there is enough diversity and originality in his corpus to insure him a permanent role in the literary histories and anthologies of the future.

Abbreviations

found in notes and bibliography not otherwise noted

BMFEA - *Bulletin of the Museum of Far Eastern Antiquities*
BSOAS - *Bulletin of the School of Oriental and African Studies, London*
ch. - *chüan*
CYYY - *Bulletin of the Institute of History and Philology, Academia Sinica*
fol. - folio page
HJAS - *Harvard Journal of Asiatic Studies*
JOS - *Journal of Oriental Studies*
OE - *Oriens Extremus*
Perspectives - *Perspectives on the T'ang,* edited by Arthur F. Wright and
    Denis Twitchett (New Haven: Yale University Press, 1973).
SPPY - *Ssu-pu pei-yao*
SPTK - *Ssu-pu ts'ung-k'an*
TP - *T'oung Pao*
YCGL - *Yearbook of Comparative and General Literature*

Notes and References

Preface

1. Quoted from a conversation with Georges Poulet recorded in *The Structuralist Controversy* (Baltimore: Johns Hopkins, 1972), p. 83.

Chapter One

1. "Die kleine Kraft, welche Noth thut, einen Kahn in den Strom hineinzustossen, soll nicht mit der Kraft dieses Stromes, der ihn fürderhin trägt, verwechselt werden: aber es geschieht fast in allen Biographien" ["Fehler der Biographen"]—my translation from Friedrich Nietzsche, "Vermischte Méinungen und Sprüche," #394, in *Menschliches Allzumenschliches*, vol. 2 (Part 4, vol. 3 of *Nietzsche Werke*, Giorgio Colli and Mazzino Montinari, eds. [Berlin: Walter de Gruyter & Co., 1967]), p. 166.

2. In establishing reign dates, Robert des Rotours, *Traité des examens* (Paris: Ernest Leroux, 1932), pp. 348–54, has been followed.

3. See vol. 17, *ch.* 244–45, pp. 7883–912 (Peking: Chung-hua shu-chü, 1956). Translations are by the author unless otherwise noted.

4. On the history of this controversy see Eugene Feifel, *Po Chü-i as a Censor* ('S-Gravenhage: Mouton and Co., 1961), pp. 43–55 and Margaret Tudor South, *Li Ho, a Scholar-official of the Yüan-ho Period (806–821)* (Adelaide: Libraries Board of South Australia, 1967), pp. 14–15 and 28–29.

5. See South, *Li Ho*, p. 28.

6. See Colin Mackerras, *The Uighur Empire According to the T'ang Dynasty Histories* (Canberra: Centre of Oriental Studies, The Australian National University, 1968), pp. 121–22 and 158.

7. On Li Tsai-i, see *Hsin T'ang-shu* (New T'ang History, hereafter *HTS*), vol. 19, *ch.* 212, p. 5978 (Peking: Chung-hua shu-chü, 1975) and *Chiu T'ang-shu* (Old T'ang History, hereafter *CTS*), vol. 14, *ch.* 180, pp. 4674–75 (Peking: Chung-hua shu-chü, 1975).

8. On this general trend, see David S. Nivison, "Protest against Conventions and Conventions of Protest," in *The Confucian Persuasion*, edited by Arthur F. Wright (Stanford: Stanford University Press, 1960), pp. 177–201; on Li Te-yü's specific contributions to this movement, see E. G. Pul-

leyblank, "Liu K'o, A Forgotten Rival of Han Yü," *Asia Major*, 7(1959), p. 146, and Robert des Rotours, *Traité des examens*, pp. 195–205.

9. Li Chung-min was apparently unaware that Sung had died in the seventh lunar month of the preceding year; see his biographies, *CTS*, vol. 13, *ch.* 167, pp. 4370–72, and *HTS*, vol. 15, *ch.* 152, pp. 4844–46.

10. For a summary of this incident, see James J. Y. Liu, *The Poetry of Li Shang-yin, Ninth-century Baroque Chinese Poet* (Chicago and London: University of Chicago Press, 1969), pp. 168–69.

11. This omen follows the report of Cheng Chu's attendance on the emperor for the first time and is clearly meant to indicate the former's malfeasance.

12. On this period, see Robert Somers, "The Collapse of the T'ang Order" (Unpublished Ph.D. dissertation, Yale University, 1975).

13. Much of the following discussion is adapted from Jacques Gernet's excellent treatment of social, political, and economic developments during the late T'ang in *La Monde chinoise* (Paris: Cobin, 1972), pp. 238ff.

14. See Gernet, *Monde*, p. 229.

15. Inaba Ichirō, "Hi Jitsu-kyu oyobi Tan-Chō-Riku shi no *Shunjū* ken-kyu" [Studies of the *Spring and Autumn Annals* by P'i Jih-hsiu and Mssrs. Tan (Chu), Chao (Kuang), and Lu (Ch'un)], in Utsunomiya Kiyoyoshi, ed., *Chugoku chuseishi kenkyu—Rikucho Sui To no shakai to bunka* (A Study of Chinese Medieval History—The Society and Culture of the Six Dynasties, Sui and T'ang) (Tokyo: Tokai University Press, 1970), pp. 389–97.

16. See Yoshikawa Kojirō, *Yüan tsa-chü yen-chiu*, Cheng Ch'ing-mao, trans. (Taipei: I-wen yin-shu-kuan, 1960), p. 4.

17. Cf. Gernet, *Monde*, p. 256.

18. Nivison, "Protest," p. 178, argues that "conservatism, a love of antiquity" may be viewed as merely a "protest against an ignoble conventionality."

19. On Liu Tsung-yüan, see William H. Nienhauser, Jr., *et al.*, *Liu Tsung-yüan* (New York: Twayne, 1973); chapter 3, "Philosophical and Intellectual Thought" (pp. 45–65) by William B. Crawford, deals especially with Liu's attitudes toward the classics.

20. See his "Pien *Lieh-tzu*" [A Critical Discussion of the *Lieh-tzu*], "*Lun-yü* pien, erh-p'ien" [Critical Discussions of *The Analects*, Two Selections], and similar essays in *ch.* 4 of his collected works, *Liu Ho-tung hsien-sheng chi* (Peking: Chung-hua shu-chü, 1960), pp. 62–72.

21. Lai Ku had something of a national reputation as an author of satiric vignettes during the early 860s, see Wu Ting-pao (870–955?), *T'ang chih yen*, *ch.* 10, fol. 7a *(SPPY)*; Sun Kuang-hsien, *Pei-meng so-yen* (Peking: Chung-hua shu-chü, 1960), p. 58; and Hsin Wen-pien, *T'ang-ts'ai tzu-chuan* (Shanghai: Ku-tien wen-hsüeh ch'u-pan-she, 1957), vol. 1, *ch.* 8, p. 134.

22. *Ch'üan T'ang wen* [Complete Prose of the T'ang; cited hereafter as

Wen] (Taipei: Hua-lien ch'u-pan-she, 1965), vol. 17, *ch.* 811, fol. 13a–b.

23. Other than the date of Ch'eng Yen's *chin-shih* success (895), nothing is known of him; cf. *Wen*, vol. 17, *ch.* 821, fol. 1a.

24. *Wen*, vol. 17, *ch.* 821, fol. 3b–4a.

25. On Wang Chao-chün, see Herbert Giles, *Biographical Dictionary* (Reprint; Taipei: Ch'eng-wen Publishing Co., 1968), p. 812 (no. 2148).

26. See Everett E. Hagen, *On the Theory of Social Change* (Homewood, Illinois: Dorsey, 1962), pp. 193–95.

27. On the development of the *tz'u*, see Glen William Baxter, "Metrical Origins of the *Tz'u*," *HJAS*, 16 (1953), pp. 108–45.

28. See South, "Li Ho and the New *Yüeh-fu* Movement," *Journal of the Oriental Society of Australia*, 4.2 (December 1966), pp. 49–61.

29. An excellent discussion of these schools is provided by Jonathan Chaves in his *Mei Yao-ch'en and the Development of Early Sung Poetry* (New York and London: Columbia, 1976), pp. 53–68.

30. These three literati have recently received a great deal of attention in the People's Republic; see, for example, *Chung-kuo wen-hsüeh-shih ch'ao* [A Draft History of Chinese Literature], edited by the Editors and Writers' Group for History of Chinese Literature Teaching Material, Chi-lin University (Ch'ang-ch'ün: Chi-lin jen-min ch'u-pan-she, 1961), vol. 2, pp. 234–40 on P'i, Tu, and Nieh and pp. 243–44 on Lo.

31. The most important sources of P'i's life are his own *P'i-tzu wen-sou* [Literary Marsh of Master P'i] (Peking: Chung-hua shu-chü, 1959); his "T'ai-hu shih hsü" [Preface to the Poems on Great Lake], in *Ch'üan T'ang shih* [Complete T'ang Poetry; hereafter *Shih*] (Taipei: Ming-lun ch'u-pan-she, 1971), vol. 9, *ch.* 610, p. 7034; Hsü Sung's (1781–1848) *Teng-k'o-chi k'ao* (Taipei: Ching-sheng wen-wu kung-ying kung-ssu, 1972), vol. 3, *ch.* 23, fol. 11b–12a, pp. 1466–67; Sun, *Pei-meng, ch.* 2, p. 7; Ch'ien I's *Nan-pu hsin-shu* (Shanghai: Shang-wu yin-shu-kuan, 1936), *ch.* 4, p. 34, and *ch.* 10, p. 105; Chi Yu-kung's *T'ang-shih chi-shih* (Taipei: Chung-hua shu-chü, 1970), *ch.* 64, pp. 964–67; Ch'en Chen-sun's *Chih-chai shu-lu chieh-t'i* (Shanghai: Commercial Press, 1939), *ch.* 16, p. 458; Chao Kung-wu's *Chün-chai tu-shu-chih* (Taipei: Kuang-wen shu-chü, 1967), vol. 3, *ch.* 16, fol. 18a–b, pp. 1079–80; Yin Chu's (1001–1046) "Ta-li-ssu ch'eng P'i Tzu-liang mu-chih" [Tablet Inscription for the Assistant in the Court of Supreme Justice, P'i Tzu-liang], *Ho-nan hsien-sheng wen-chi, ch.* 15, fol. 5a–6b *(SPTK);* Lu Yu's (1125–1210), *Lao-hsüeh-an pi-chi* (Shanghai: Commercial Press, 1936), *ch.* 10, pp. 97–98; Fan Ch'eng-ta's (1126–1193) *Wu-chün chih*, *ch.* 12, fol. 3a *(Shou-shan-ko ts'ung-shu);* and Hsin Wen-fang, *T'ang ts'ai-tzu chuan* (Peking: Chung-hua shu-chü, 1965), *ch.* 8, pp. 143–45.

For modern studies on P'i see the Selected Bibliography, section 1 of the Secondary Sources.

32. In "Wen-chung-tzu pei-hsü" [Preface to the Funerary Inscription of Master Wen-chung], *Literary Marsh, ch.* 4, p. 38, P'i states that he was

born some 250 years after Wang T'ung (584–618)—i.e., *ca.* 834. Though
various other dates have also been proposed, the question is moot, and 834
seems to correspond closely to later developments in P'i's life. This date,
moreover, has been adopted by the editors of the new edition of the *Tz'u-
hai* (Shanghai: Chung-hua shu-chü, 1961), Section 10, p. 36. The major
Western-language source, Donald A. Holzman's notice in *Dictionary of
Oriental Literatures* (New York: Basic Books, 1974), vol. 1, p. 140, is certainly in error in listing P'i's birthdate as "c. 843."

33. See Yen Keng-wang, "T'ang-tai p'ien," in *Chung-kuo li-shih ti-li,*
Shih Chang-ju, ed. (Taipei: Chung-hua wen-hua ch'u-pan shih-yen wei-
yüan-hui, 1954), vol. 2, p. 18. The population figure listed here is based on
5.5 individuals per household and shows an increase of 100 percent since
the mid-eighth century (*ibid.*, p. 17). For a description of developments in
this area during the T'ang, see Wang Gungwu, "The Middle Yangtze in
T'ang Politics," in *Perspectives*, pp. 197–230.

34. See *Chung-kuo wen-hsüeh*, Editors and Writers, ed. vol. 1, p. 4.

35. See Yang Tsung-shih, ed., *Hsiang-chou hsien-chih* (Taipei: Taiwan
hsüeh-sheng shu-chü, 1969), vol. 3, *ch.* 7, fol. 32b, p. 1224.

36. *Ibid.*, vol. 3, *ch.* 7, fol. 4a, p. 1161.

37. "P'i-tzu shih-lu" [A Genealogy of Master P'i], *Literary Marsh, ch.*
10, pp. 125–26. On P'i's posterity, see Yin Chu, "Mu-chih."

38. P'i Ch'u has no extant biography.

39. See his biographies in the *Pei Ch'i shu* (Peking: Chung-hua shu-chü,
1972), vol. 2, *ch.* 41, pp. 536–38 and *Pei shih, ch.* 53, fol. 23a–24b *(Po-na).*

40. Hsü Sung, in the *Teng-k'o*, vol. 3, *ch.* 27, fol. 32b, p. 1796, notes
only that P'i Hang-hsiu was a *ming-ching* examination graduate and that he
held office.

41. See Twitchett's "Chinese Social History from the Seventh to the
Tenth Centuries," *Past and Present*, 35 (1966), p. 49, on the *wang-tsu.*

42. See *"P'i-tzu wen-sou* hsü," *Literary Marsh*, p. ii.

43. *Ibid., ch.* 10, p. 125.

44. See Etienne Balazs' definition of this class based upon their
economic basis, their uniform style of life, their traditionalist outlook, their
upbringing, their notion of honor, and their literacy in his "Significant
Aspects of Chinese Society," in *Chinese Civilization and Bureaucracy* (New
Haven and London: Yale University Press, 1964), p. 6. P'i fits all the re-
quirements stipulated for membership in this class.

45. See, for example, Robert Nisbet, "History and Sociology," in *Tradition and Revolt* (New York: Random House, 1968), p. 92.

46. *Ibid.*, p. 95.

47. Particularly as they are presented and applied in Gail Sheehy's
interesting *Passages, Predictable Crises of Adult Life* (New York: E. P.
Dutton, 1976).

48. This mountain takes its name from two stone-carved deer placed on

either side of a path leading to the temple built by the Marquis of Hsiang-yang about the year 500; see *Hsiang-yang-chi*, as cited in Morohashi Tet-suji, *Daikanwa jiten* (Tokyo: Taishūkan shoten, 1959), vol. 12, p. 13504, gloss 47586.135.3 (Original text not available).

49. A type of hat worn by a hermit, especially typical of the Hsiang-yang area; see Ch'eng Ta-ch'ang (1123–1195), *Yen fan-lu*, *ch.* 10, fol. 2b (*Hsüeh-chin t'ao-yüan* edition).

50. Wang Su (d. 256) was known as "clepsydra cup" because of his ability to consume a ladle of wine with a single swallow; see *Lo-yang chia-lan chi*, *ch.* 3, fol. 4a ('SPPY).

51. *Shih*, vol. 9, *ch.* 608, p. 7022.

52. See, for example, *Hsiang-yang hsien-chih*, vol. 3, *ch.* 7, fol. 32a.

53. *Shih*, vol. 9, *ch.* 608, p. 7022.

54. Lü Ssu-mien, *Sui T'ang Wu-tai shih* (Shanghai: Chung-hua shu-chü, 1959), vol. 2, p. 1273.

55. One such mentor, Lu Heng, had five hundred students; *ibid.*, p. 1271.

56. *Ibid.*, pp. 1263–64.

57. Pulleyblank, "Liu K'o," pp. 157–58, n. 63.

58. See Nivison, "Protest," p. 178, on this conflict.

59. On the possible contemporary symbolic meaning of these insects, see the text and commentary of Liu Yü-hsi's poem, "Mosquitoes," in *Chinese Literature*, 1975, no. 6, p. 88 and p. 97; and also Chaves on Mei Yao-ch'en's "Swarming Mosquitoes," in *Mei Yao-ch'en*, pp. 188–91.

60. *Shih*, vol. 9, *ch.* 608, p. 7022.

61. Cf. Ma's biography, *Hou Han shu* (Peking: Chung-hua shu-chü, 1965), vol. 7, *ch.* 60A, p. 1972.

62. Fan Ch'eng-ta, *Wu-chün chih*, *ch.* 12, fol. 3b, however, says that this work was completed in 869. It is likely that most of it was written while P'i was at Deer-Gate and that he merely edited these writings while in Soochow.

63. *Shih*, vol. 9, *ch.* 615, p. 7093.

64. This expression is from *Chuang-tzu* (*A Concordance to Chuang Tzu* [Cambridge, Mass.: Harvard University Press, 1956], p. 69, xxv. 4); it has also been glossed as "self-reliance," suggesting conceit.

65. See his biographies, adjacent to those of Tu Ju-hui, in *CTS*, vol. 7, *ch.* 66' pp. 2459–67, and *HTS*, vol. 6, *ch.* 96' pp. 3853–57.

66. See *CTS*, vol. 7, *ch.* 66, pp. 2467–73, and *HTS*, vol. 6, *ch.* 96, pp. 3858–60.

67. See *HTS*, vol. 16, *ch.* 154, pp. 4863–73, and *CTS*, vol. 11, *ch.* 133, pp. 3661–76.

68. See *HTS*, vol. 18, *ch.* 196, pp. 5603–4.

69. See *CTS*, vol. 15, *ch.* 190B, pp. 5050–51, and *HTS*, vol. 18, ch. 194, pp. 5563–65.

70. See *CTS*, vol. 15, *ch.* 190C, pp. 5053–54, and *HTS*, vol. 18, *ch.* 202, pp. 5762–64.

71. See *CTS*, vol. 13, *ch.* 166, pp. 4341–58, and *HTS*, vol. 14, *ch.* 119, pp. 4300–305.

72. *Literary Marsh, ch.* 10, p. 111.

73. See *T'ang hui yao* (Shanghai: Commercial Press, 1936), *ch.* 77, p. 1402, and the original text of this memorial in *Literary Marsh, ch.* 9, pp. 95–96.

74. Among numerous works, Li Shen-ssu's (fl. 870) *Hsü Meng-tzu* [Sequel to Mencius] might be cited. Lin was a contemporary of P'i and was also courted by Huang Ch'ao, but his refusal to join the rebel leader resulted in his demise.

75. In *Literary Marsh*, pp. 28–29 and 23–24 respectively.

76. In "P'i-tzu shih-lu," *Literary Marsh, ch.* 10, p. 126, P'i states that his clan has "farmed Ching-ling," referring to Ching-ling Commandery, a part of Ying-chou.

77. During his stay with Li, P'i wrote the "T'ung-hsüan-tzu Hsi-pin-t'ing chi" [Record of the Refuge-for-a-Guest Pavilion of the Master who Penetrates the Dark], *Literary Marsh, ch.* 7, pp. 77–78, in which he indicates that Li had wanted him to stay in P'eng-tse (ten miles southeast of modern P'eng-tse County in Kiangsi Province).

78. *Literary Marsh, ch.* 7, pp. 76–77.

79. See Li Fang, *T'ai-p'ing kuang-chi* (Peking: Jen-min wen-hsüeh ch'u-pan-she, 1959), vol. 3, *ch.* 257, pp. 1999–2000. *Ch'u-t'ou*, "to stick out the head," may also suggest emerging and becoming successful in society. The passage goes on to record a poem which Kuei Jen-shao's sons wrote about a piece of skin (a homonym for P'i's surname), mocking P'i in retaliation; see also an abbreviated version of this anecdote in Sun, *Pei-meng, ch.* 7, p. 60.

80. See "T'ai-hu shih hsü," *Shih*, vol. 9, *ch.* 610, p. 7034.

81. The inscription is found in *Literary Marsh, ch.* 4, p. 45. On provincial candidates *(kung-shih)*, see des Rotours, *Traité*, p. 169, n. 3.

82. See P'i's preface to *Literary Marsh*, p. 1.

83. See *T'ang chih yen, ch.* 3, fol. 5b. On some of the pagentry of this era, see *ibid., ch.* 15, fol. 4b.

84. *Shih*, vol. 10, *ch.* 696, p. 8006.

85. In *Shih-chi*, vol. 7, *ch.* 106, pp. 2825 and 2834 (Peking: Chung-hua shu-chü, 1959).

86. Robin Yates, who is currently completing a translation of Wei Chuang's poetic corpus, believes this poem was written in 881 while Wei was in hiding from Huang Ch'ao in Ch'ang-an. He points out that "blossoms from the grotto" may also refer to beautiful women, noting that one finds similar wording in Wei's "On Visiting Yang-chou" (*Shih*, vol. 10, *ch.* 697, p. 8021):

> In those years people were not yet used to the sword—
> every place green towers [in which courtesans dwelt],
>   every night songs;
> Blossoms open in grottoes, spring days forever,
> as the moon brightens the fines breezes seem to multiply
>   over my robes.

Moreover, according to Yates references in Wei's extant poetry to T'ao Ch'ien or Lao-tzu are exceedingly uncommon.

87. Ling-hu T'ao was an especially powerful figure during the reign of Hsüan-tsung (r. 847–860); see his biography in *HTS*, vol. 16, *ch.* 166, pp. 5101–3, and Somers, "Collapse," p. 4. He was the patron of Li Shang-yin (see Huang Ch'ing-shih, "Li Shang-yin yü Ling-hu fu-tzu" [Li Shang-yin and the Ling-hu's, Father and Son], in *T'ang-shih yen-chiu lun-wen-chi* [Peking: Jen-min ch'u-pan-she, 1959], pp. 353–59) and was one of the major leaders of the Niu Seng-ju faction during this period. P'i apparently met him as he was returning via Hsiang-chou to the capital around 850; cf. *Shih*, vol. 9, *ch.* 613, p. 7068. It is also interesting to note that Shou-chou, where P'i compiled the *Literary Marsh* in 866, was the prefecture closest to Ch'ang-an under Ling-hu's jurisdiction. On P'i's visit see "*Sung-ling chi* hsü," *Sung-ling chi*, fol. 3a (*Hu-pei hsien-sheng i-shu* edition).

88. See Hsiao Ti-fei's "Chiao-tien *P'i-tzu wen-sou shou-ming–chien lun yu-kuan P'i Jih-hsiu chu wen-t'i*" [Some Explanatory Comments on the Collated and Punctuated Edition of *Master P'i's Literary Marsh*, with a Discussion of Several Questions Concerning P'i Jih-hsiu], *Wen-shih-che*, January 1958, pp. 3707–13.

89. See Wang Te-chen, *Lo Yin nien-p'u* (Shanghai: Commercial Press, 1937), p. 17.

90. See *Nan-pu hsin-shu*, *ch.* 1, p. 23: "Since the T'ai-chung era [847–859], when the Ministry of Rites posts the list of examination graduates, they pick two or three persons annually with uncommon surnames . . . calling them the 'flowers of the examination lists' [*pang-hua*]." On P'i's performance in the examinations, see also Hsü Sung, *Teng-k'o*, vol. 3, *ch.* 23, fol. 11b–12a, pp. 1466–67.

91. The anecdote concerning Ts'ui (*T'ai-p'ing kuang-chi*, *ch.* 265, p. 2082) is of interest. There is no other biographical source for Ts'ui other than this passage. His father, Ts'ui Liao, suffers the same fate. Since one is told here that Ts'ui is of a good family, he may have belonged to the Ch'ing-ho Ts'ui clan and thus have been related to P'i's patron and superior in Soochow, Ts'ui P'u. At any rate, during a spring celebration at the Winding River early in 868 following the examination success of both Ts'ui and P'i, the latter fell into a drunken stupor amidst his book satchels and luggage. Ts'ui, seeing him, decided to ridicule this "special graduate" (see note 90). When P'i's servants wanted to wake their master, Ts'ui dissuaded them, saying: "He's just in a clan gathering!" referring to the leather (*p'i*)

bags and satchels. This riposte then became the talk of the capital.

92. The incident involving Cheng Yü is recorded in Sun, *Pei-meng, ch.* 2, p. 7. Cheng was an eccentric character who loved to attract attention (see, for example, *T'ang chih yen, ch.* 20, fol. 5a–b). He was from the Kuang-chou (Canton) area and most of his career was spent as a military governor in the South. Called to court in 867 as a reward for his loyal service, he was sent out again immediately after the examinations to become Prefect of Kuang-chou the following year. In later years he became a chief minister; see his biography in Ch'en Ch'ang-chai, *et al., Kuang-tung t'ung-chih* (Taipei: Hua-wen shu-chü, 1968), vol. 7, *ch.* 268, fol. 29a–30a, pp. 4441–42; vol. 1, *ch.* 13, fol. 10b, p. 263; and vol. 1, *ch.* 13, fol. 11b, p. 264.

93. He continued to communicate with Sung K'ou, cf. *Shih*, vol. 9, *ch.* 612, p. 7064.

94. The recorder was one of several "officers" appointed by the highest ranking graduate to serve during the postexamination festivities, see des Rotours, *Traité,* p. 281.

95. *Shih,* vol. 9, *ch.* 613, p. 7068.

96. See note 91.

97. On this holiday, see Alsace Yen, "The Parry-Lord Theory Applied to Vernacular Chinese Stories," *JAOS*, 95(1975), pp. 407–8, n. 11; and W. Eberhard, "Das Fest des Kaltessens," in *Lokalkulturen im alten China* (Leiden: Brill, 1942), pp. 36–51.

98. See note 90.

99. See the poem addressed by P'i to the Vice-president of the Ministry of the Army, *Shih,* vol. 9, *ch.* 613, p. 7067. P'i may have taken both examinations during the same year, as Liu Shen-ssu did; cf. *Teng-k'o,* vol. 3, *ch.* 23, fol. 14b–15a. On this examination itself, see des Rotours, *Traité,* pp. 220–21.

100. Some accounts disagree here and feel that P'i did win a position at this time; see Miao Yüeh, "P'i Jih-hsiu te shih-chi ssu-hsiang chi ch'i tso-p'in" [Biographical Facts, Thought, and Works of P'i Jih-hsiu], in *T'ang-shih yen-chiu lun-wen-chi* (Peking: Jen-min wen-hsüeh ch'u-pan-she, 1959), pp. 375–76.

101. See P'i's poem to Sung K'ou, "Chiang-nan shu-ch'ing erh-shih yün," *Shih,* vol. 9, *ch.* 612, p. 7064.

102. See Miao Yüeh, "P'i Jih-hsiu," p. 376.

103. P'i himself says he came to Wu (Soochow) to avoid troops; see Chou Lien-kuan, "P'i Jih-hsiu te sheng-p'ing chi ch'i chu-tso," *Ling-nan hsüeh-pao,* 12.1(June 1952), pp. 113–44.

104. See "T'ai-hu shih hsü," *Shih,* vol. 9, *ch.* 610, p. 7034.

105. There is reason to believe that P'i and Ts'ui were previously acquainted. Ts'ui Lu, who also came to Soochow during this period and who had taken the examinations with P'i in 866, was possibly a relative of P'u.

Moreover, P'i's "A Fisherman's Family at the Western-border Mountain Quai," a part of his *Literary Marsh* corpus (*ch.* 10, p. 124), seems to have been written in the Soochow area, suggesting the possibility that P'i had already visited Soochow before he took the examinations.

106. For biographical material, see *HTS*, vol. 18, *ch.* 196, pp. 5612–13; "Su-chou fu," *ch.* 4, fol. 8b and *ch.* 2, fol. 8b–9a in *Chia-ch'ing chung-hsiu i-t'ung-chih (SPTK)*; Sun, *Pei-meng, ch.* 6, p. 52; *T'ang ts'ai-tzu chuan, ch.* 8, fol. 11b (Taipei: Kuang-wen shu-chü, 1969); Chi, *T'ang-shih chi-shih*, vol. 2, *ch.* 64, pp. 961–63; and Lu's autobiographical pieces, such as "Fu-li hsien-sheng chuan," in *Wen-yüan ying-hua* (Taipei: Hua-wen shu-chü, 1965), vol. 10, *ch.* 796, fol. 6a–8a, pp. 5021–22.

107. See "Erh yu shih hsü" [Preface to the Poems of Two Journeys], *Shih*, vol. 9, *ch.* 609, p. 7028.

108. See "Ou-liu Yang Chen-wen . . .," *ibid.*, *ch.* 614, p. 7090.

109. According to *Lo Yin nien-p'u* (pp. 33–36), Lo was in Ch'ang-an for much of this period.

110. Hsiao, "Chiao-tien," p. 3708.

111. See Chou Lien-kuan, "P'i Jih-hsiu te sheng-p'ing chi ch'i tso-p'in" [P'i Jih-hsiu's Life and Works], *Ling-nan hsüeh-pao*, 12.1(June 1952), pp. 113 and 120.

112. See, for example, Ts'ui Lu's only extant poem, *Shih*, vol. 10, *ch.* 631, p. 7238.

113. On this group, see Chou, "P'i Jih-hsiu," p. 131; see also their works in *Sung-ling chi*, in *Shih*, vol. 9, *ch.* 631, and the miscellaneous biographical information in *T'ang-shih chi-shih, ch.* 64.

114. See Austin Warren and René Wellek, *Theory of Literature* (New York: Harcourt, Brace and World, 1966), p. 101.

115. See Jung's comments cited in Gail Sheehy, *Passages*, p. 273. See also Erikson, *Young Man Luther* (New York: Norton, 1958), p. 43. These observations are not meant to claim that P'i fits European norms, but merely to suggest that "adult psychological stages" are to be expected.

116. P'i wrote numerous poems on Hsi Shih during his years in Soochow; see chapter 4.

117. See Lu Kuei-meng's poem congratulating P'i on his wedding, *Shih*, vol. 9, *ch.* 625, p. 7180.

118. *Shih*, vol. 9, *ch.* 615, p. 7093.

119. Again scholars differ as to P'i's activities at this time. This study follows Chou Lien-kuan.

120. On P'i Kuang-yeh, see Yin Chu, "Mu-chih"; Fan Chiung-lin, *Wu-yüeh pei-shih, ch.* 3, fol. 3b–4a *(SPTK)*; and Fan Ch'eng-ta, *Wu-chün chih, ch.* 25, fol. 1b.

121. See des Rotours, *Traité*, p. 248. This position was often given to recent examination graduates.

122. See Chou, "P'i Jih-hsiu," p. 123.

123. According to Chao, *Chün-chai*, vol. 3, *ch.* 16, fol. 18a.

124. On these theories, see Chou, "P'i Jih-hsiu," pp. 124–28, and Miao, "P'i Jih-hsiu," pp. 397ff.

125. On Huang Ch'ao's campaign routes for this period, see the map in Hou Chung-i, *Huang Ch'ao ch'i-i* (Peking: Chung-hua shu-chü, 1974), between pp. 20 and 21. On Huang Ch'ao, see also Lin Yen-ch'ing, *Huang Ch'ao* (Shanghai: Shanghai jen-min ch'u-pan-she, 1962), and Howard Levy, *Biography of Huang Ch'ao* (Berkeley and Los Angeles: University of California Press, 1955). His troops occupied Loyang without a battle on December 22, 880, and took Ch'ang-an on January 8, 881.

126. In Frederick Wakeman's terminology, P'i would be considered a "social reformer" who joined a "social bandit"; see his "Popular Movements in Chinese History," *JAS*, 36.2 (February 1977), pp. 201–37.

127. See *CTS*, vol. 16, *ch.* 200B, p. 5392.

128. Translated by Lionel Giles, *TP*, 24 (1926), pp. 338–39.

129. See "Hsin-ch'eng san-lao Tung-kung tsan," *Wen-sou*, *ch.* 4, p. 46.

130. See Levy, *Huang Ch'ao*, pp. 28–31.

131. See *ibid.*, p. 31, and note 133.

132. Giles, p. 342.

133. See Ssu-ma Kuang, *Tzu-chih t'ung-chien*, *ch.* 254, fol. 10b *(SPPY)*, and Levy, *Huang Ch'ao*, p. 35.

134. "Hi Jitsu-kyu ni tsuite," in *Zen Tōshi zakki* (Kyoto: Ibundo shoten, 1969), p. 82.

135. *Shih*, vol. 9, *ch.* 615, p. 7099.

136. *Nan-pu hsin-shu*, *ch.* 4, p. 34. Such analyses were effected by ingeniously dividing up the Chinese characters in question into a set of their component parts—in this case Ch'ao (radical 47 [*ch'uan*, "stream"] above the character for "fruit" [*kuo*]). See also Levy's explanation, *Huang Ch'ao*, p. 75, n. 151.

137. Giles, p. 344.

138. *T'ai-p'ing kuang-chi*, *ch.* 265, p. 2083. Liu's biography is in *HTS*, vol. 16, *ch.* 160, p. 4970, and *CTS*, vol. 12, *ch.* 153, p. 4086. Since Liu was examiner in 868 (see *Teng-k'o*, *ch.* 23, fol. 13a, p. 1469) and had been appointed Military Governor of Ou-yüeh in 866, this meeting seems to have taken place at about this time, probably after P'i's failure in the examination of 866.

139. See his biography in *Hou Han shu*, vol. 9, *ch.* 80B, pp. 2652–56.

140. *Shih*, vol. 9, *ch.* 613, p. 7065.

141. On Ts'ao see "Wu-ti chi" [Annals of Emperor Wu], *San-kuo chih* (Peking: Chung-hua shu-chü, 1959), vol. 1, *ch.* 1, pp. 1–55.

Chapter Two

1. New York: Oxford University Press, 1953.

2. Chicago and London: University of Chicago Press, 1962.

3. Chicago and London: University of Chicago Press, 1975.

4. One might note that yet another relationship exists between the four literary poles Liu has posited: that of reader → writer. The entire school of literary reception would seem to be based on this relationship.

5. *Theories*, p. 14.

6. *Ibid.*, p. 111.

7. *Ibid.*, p. 127.

8. Most influential in the literature (the rise of the *tz'u*) and literary criticism (works such as Han Wo's [844–923] preface to his own writings, "*Hsiang-lien chi* tzu-hsü") of this period.

9. *Chüan* 4, p. 22 in a biographical note to Lu Kuei-meng (Hong Kong: Shang-wu yin-shu-kuan, n. d.).

10. See his *Chung-kuo wen-hsüeh p'i-p'ing shih* (Shang-hai: Ku-tien wen-hsüeh ch'u-pan-she, 1957), vol. 2, pp. 174–175.

11. "Hi Jitsu-kyu," pp. 95–108.

12. See "Fu-tan ta hsüeh Chung-wen hsi Chung-kuo wen-hsüeh p'i-p'an," *Wen-hsüeh i-ch'an* in *Kuang-ming jih-pao*, September 11, 1960, p. 4.

13. See his "P'i Jih-hsiu," pp. 386–89.

14. His praise for Li Shang-yin and Wei Ying-wu as the best near-contemporary poets in the preface to the *Pine Knoll Anthology* (see chapter 4) and his account of poetic history in the "Preface to the *Poetry in Miscellaneous Forms*" (see Chapter 4) are illustrations of this conception.

15. P'i's "Ch'i-ai shih" [Seven Beloved] series may be based upon Tu Fu's "Pa–ai shih" [Eight to be Pitied]; see *A Concordance to the Poems of Tu Fu* (Taipei: Chinese Materials and Research Aids Service Center, 1966), vol. 2, pp. 200–215.

16. See "Li Han-lin," *Shih*, vol. 9, *ch.* 608, p. 7018.

17. *Literary Marsh*, *ch.* 5, pp. 56–57.

18. *Ibid.*, *ch.* 8, p. 80.

19. On P'i's work on the *Spring and Autumn Annals*, see chapter 4.

20. Hsiao Chüeh (fl. 550–560) was the son of Hsiao Yeh; see Chüeh's biography in *Pei Ch'i shih* [History of the Northern Ch'i], *ch.* 45, fol. 34b–35a *(Po-na)*.

21. This is the second couplet of Hsiao's "Ch'iu ssu" [Autumn Thoughts] in Ting Fu-pao, *Ch'üan Pei-Ch'i shih* [Complete Poetry of the Northern Ch'i] in *Ch'üan Han San-kuo Chin Nan-pei ch'ao shih* (Peking: Chung-hua shu-chü, 1959), vol. 2, p. 1521.

22. This couplet of Meng Hao-jan seems to have surpassed its context, for the rest of the poem is lost, cf. *Shih*, vol. 3, *ch.* 160, p. 1669.

23. *Literary Marsh*, *ch.* 7, pp. 76–77.

24. Hsiao's poem is included in the *Yü-t'ai hsin-yung*, which is not one of the works with which T'ang literati were most familiar.

25. P'i does not state that he feels Meng was consciously reacting to such

lines, but he does imply that they were a part of Meng's "mental corpus" and that they influenced his work.

26. "Overcoming the ancients" is, for example, a phrase which suggests the theories of Harold Bloom.

27. Referring to the most revered genres and those found in the *Book of Documents*.

28. The six modes are *fu, pi, hsing, feng, ya,* and *sung*. See also P'i's "Preface to the *Pine Knoll Anthology*," in chapter 2, p. 46.

29. This line is built about a play on Po's style, Lo-t'ien, and reads literally, "He *took joy in nature* [Lo-t'ien] and alone was contented [not to strive]."

30. "Put it aside" alludes to "Ts'ai ling" [Mao number 125] in the *Book of Poetry*, and refers to "putting aside" slanderous stories.

31. "Two side-apartments" or the royal harems. Used here perhaps *pars pro toto* for the palace.

32. Whistling is a typical recluse behavior. The three rivers, Ching, Wei, and Lo, refer synecdochically to the capital.

33. *Shih,* vol. 9, *ch.* 608, p. 7018. The turtle and the mirror are both models for official behavior, the former because it was employed in divination and the latter since it was symbolic of the past as a guide to the present.

34. Po Chü-i divided his own works into four categories, and claimed that "satirical" verse *(feng-yü)* and poems "expressing his own feelings" *(hsien-shih)* were the most important. This classification is discussed in Po's "Yü Yüan Chiu shu" [Letter to Yüan Chen], *Po-shih ch'ang-ch'ing chi, ch.* 28, pp. 143–44 *(SPTK)*. The subject of Po's evaluations of Hsü and Chang was also discussed by P'i's contemporary Fan Lu (fl. 877) in his *Yün-hsi yu-i* (Shanghai: Chung-hua shu-chü, 1959), *ch.* 3, pp. 30–32, and by Chi Yu-kung in *T'ang shih chi-shih,* vol. 2, *ch.* 52, pp. 789–95.

35. *Wen,* vol. 17, *ch.* 797, fol. 10b–11b, pp. 10545–46.

36. See Sun Wang, *Yüan Tz'u-shan nien-p'u* (Peking: Chung-hua shu-chü, 1962), pp. 23–24.

37. P'i often mentions the six modes of poetry; see for example, his "Grand Tutor Po" translated above in this chapter.

38. *Literary Marsh,* p. ii.

39. See *A Concordance to Yi Ching* (Peking: Harvard-Yenching Institute, 1935), p. 49.

40. "These writings," for example, is from the *Analects,* 9.5.

41. On this series, see William H. Nienhauser, Jr., " 'Twelve Poems Propagating the Music Bureau Ballad': A Series of *Yüeh-fu* by Yüan Chieh," in *Critical Essays on Chinese Literature* (Hong Kong: Chinese University of Hong Kong Press, 1976), pp. 135–46.

42. *Literary Marsh, ch.* 10, p. 115.

43. *Ibid., ch.* 3, p. 24.

44. These lines are from the second stanza of Mao number 298, "Yu pi." The translation is Arthur Waley's, *The Book of Songs* (New York: Grove, 1960), p. 224.

45. From Mao number 17, "Hsing lu." The translation is based on Bernhard Karlgren, *The Book of Odes* (Stockholm: The Museum of Far Eastern Antiquities, 1950), p. 10.

46. From Mao number 3; Karlgren, p. 3.

47. From Mao number 131; Karlgren, p. 84.

48. From Mao number 251; Karlgren, p. 208.

49. From the third of three poems entitled "Yü Su Wu shih," in Shen Te-ch'ien, *Ku-shih yüan* (Hong Kong: Chung-hua shu-chü, 1973), *ch.* 2, fol. 8B, p. 56.

50. From "Po-liang shih," *ibid., ch.* 2, fol. 42, p. 47.

51. I.e., on the south bank of the lower reaches of the Yangtze around modern Nanking where the Eastern Chin set up its capital in 317. This passage generally refers to those poets of the Southern Dynasties, 317–589.

52. See Mao number 26, "Po chou."

53. On this passage, see Chow Tse-tsung, "Early History of the Chinese Word *Shih* (Poetry)," in *Wen-lin* (Madison: University of Wisconsin, 1968), pp. 152–53. The translation is that of Chow Tse-tsung.

54. The following passage is structured according to Tung Chung-shu's precepts of the transformations of *ch'i*; see Tzey-yueh Tain, "Tung Chung-shu's System of Thought, Its Sources and Its Influence on Han Scholars," (unpublished Ph.D. dissertation, University of California, Los Angeles, 1974), pp. 83–85.

55. Hsi-tzu is Hsi Shih, the renowned beauty who was used as a political pawn in the fifth-century B.C. warfare between the states of Wu and Yüeh (see chapter 4). Tun Ch'ia was a homely woman whose virtue attracted her ruler; see *Lü-shih ch'un-ch'iu, ch.* 14, fol. 20a–b *(SPTK).*

56. On Cook Ting, see *Chuang Tzu*, Burton Watson, trans. (New York: Columbia University Press, 1968), pp. 50–51. Wheelwright Pien is also the subject of a passage in *Chuang Tzu* (Watson's translation, pp. 152–53). *Hu-pen* ("tiger routers") were soldiers; see Legge, *The Chinese Classics*, vol. 3, p. 549. "The ax of Ying" is Carpenter Shih, again in Watson, *Chuang Tzu*, p. 269. All are traditional examples of "natural talent."

57. The Duke of Chou served as regent during the minority of his nephew, King Ch'eng. No record of this poem has been located.

58. On the relationship between Yin and the Earl, see Yin's poem, "Sung Kao," Mao number 259 in the *Book of Poetry*. There is no record of a poem by the Earl.

59. It has not been possible to identify this individual.

60. The translation here is tentative.

61. There is a strange error here, possibly that of a copyist or editor, for P'i himself was certainly aware that Lu Kuei-meng had not passed the *chin-shih* examination.

62. *Wen*, vol. 17, *ch.* 79b, fol. 21a–23a. The text presented in the *Wen* and translated here is incomplete, cf. the much longer version in the *Pine Knoll Anthology* itself. The translation is based on the *Wen* text, but variants from the *Pine Knoll Anthology* have been taken into consideration throughout.

63. The major "borrowing" is the discussion of the traditional line lengths and examples; see Chih Yü, *Wen-chang*, p. 265.

64. Cf. Ts'ao P'i's "Tien-lun lun'wen," translated by Ronald Miao in his "Literary Criticism at the End of the Eastern Han," *Literature East and West*, 16 (1972), pp. 1013–34.

65. It is perhaps of significance that P'i, known for his arrogance, omits in his citation a passage on restraining hubris. Translation according to James Legge, *The Shoo King*, vol. 3 of *The Chinese Classics* (Reprint; Taipei: Chin-hsüeh shu-chü, 1969), pp. 47–48.

66. See *ch.* 6, fol. 11b *(SPTK)*—my translation.

67. See Li's biography, *Han shu* (Peking: Chung-hua shu-chü, 1962), vol. 8, *ch.* 93, pp. 3725–26.

68. "Bell songs and drums and pipes" indicate military music. The "duster dances" originated in the Wu area during the Six Dynasties (first mention is in the *Chin shu*). The *yü* and its antiphon were developed during the Han dynasty (see Ts'ao Pao's biography, *Hou Han-shu*, vol. 5, *ch.* 35, p. 1201.

69. The "Musical Treatises" made up one of the original eight treatises of the *Shih-chi*. The text was lost and partially reconstructed from citations in other works.

70. *Shih*, vol. 9, *ch.* 616, pp. 7101–2.

71. "Writings of a Recluse at Deer-Gate, section 3," *Literary Marsh*, p. 99.

Chapter Three

1. *Ch.* 9, pp. 97–107.

2. See Arthur Waley's translation of 14.24 in *The Analects of Confucius* [hereafter *Analects*] (New York: Vintage, 1938), p. 187.

3. This passage remains unclear.

4. Cf. *Mencius*, 4.A.9 and 2.B.2, respectively (D. C. Lau, translator [Baltimore: Penguin, 1970], pp. 121–2 and 85–7).

5. Waley, *Analects*, 1.1, p. 83.

6. Waley, *Analects*, 1.4, p. 84.

7. Waley, *Analects*, 8.2, p. 132.

8. Waley, *Analects*, 17.8, p. 212.

9. Waley, *Analects*, 9.6.

10. *The I Ching,* "Hsi-tz'u," pt. 1, *ch.* 8.4 translated by Cary F. Baynes from the German of Richard Wilhelm (Princeton: Princeton University Press, 1967), p. 304.

11. Cf. Waley, *Analects,* 19.25 (pp. 229–30) and 1.14 (p. 87).

12. Waley, *Analects,* 17.13, p. 213.

13. Lau, *Mencius,* 7.2.37, p. 203.

14. *Ibid.,* 4.A.1, p. 118.

15. See the quotation attributed to Teng Hsi, a minister of Cheng during the Spring and Autumn era, in *T'ai-p'ing yü-lan* (Taipei: Shang-wu yin-shu-kuan, 1968), vol. 1, *ch.* 80, fol. 8a, p. 504.

16. See Watson, *Chuang-tzu,* p. 366.

17. Paraphrasing *Analects,* 15.8; see Waley, p. 195.

18. *Literary Marsh, ch.* 3, pp. 26–27.

19. See *Kuan-tzu,* vol. 1, *ch.* 11, fol. 11a–12 *(SPPY).*

20. See Legge, *The Chinese Classics,* vol. 5, pp. 403–4.

21. Lau, *Mencius,* 3.A.4, p. 101.

22. *Literary Marsh, ch.* 6, pp. 60–61.

23. *Hsün-tzu chien-chu* (Shanghai: Shanghai jen-min ch'u-pan-she, 1974), p. 178; translated by Wing-Tsit Chan in *A Source Book in Chinese Philosophy* (Princeton: Princeton University Press, 1963), p. 118.

24. Legge, *The Chinese Classics,* vol. 1, p. 357 and p. 371.

25. Lau, *Mencius,* 7.B.14, p. 196.

26. Ts'ui Ch'ü may be the same man depicted in a very brief biographical note in *CTS,* vol. 9, *ch.* 91, p. 2935, and *HTS,* vol. 14, *ch.* 120, p. 4318. If so, P'i was probably paid by the family to write this biography, since this Ts'ui Ch'ü died *ca.* 750.

27. On the meaning of "trustworthiness" *(hsin),* see D. C. Lau, "Translating Philosophical Works in Classical Chinese—Some Difficulties," in *The Art and Profession of Translation,* edited by T. C. Lai (Hong Kong: Hong Kong Translation Society, 1977), pp. 53–55.

28. *Literary Marsh, ch.* 8, pp. 83–84.

29. It was in Shou that P'i completed the *Wen-sou* in 866.

30. P'i has a prose-poem on this mountain at the beginning of the *Literary Marsh, ch.* 1, p. 1.

31. Tossing stones seems to have been an ancient form of competition through which soldiers could be evaluated, see *Shih-chi,* vol. 7, *ch.* 73, p. 2341.

32. Southeast of modern T'ung-ch'eng County in Anhwei Province.

33. *Literary Marsh, ch.* 8, pp. 84–86.

34. See biographical discussion in Chapter I.

35. This allusion remains obscure.

36. *Literary Marsh, ch.* 7, pp. 70–71.

37. This classification varies, but here follows the nearest contemporary account, Ssu-ma Chen's "San-huang pen-chi" [Basic Annals of the Three

Emperors] which was incorporated into the *Shih-chi* during the T'ang dynasty (p. 33 [*Po-na*]).

38. This scheme also admits of several interpretations; cf. Morohashi, *Daikanwa*, vol. 1, p. 501, gloss number 257.848.1.

39. This is a quotation from Yang Hsiung's (53 B.C.–A.D. 18) *Fa-yen*; see Wang Jung-pao, *Fa-yen i-shu* (Taipei: Shih-chieh shu-chü, 1962), vol. 1, *ch.* 4, fol. 13b, p. 132.

40. *Literary Marsh, ch.* 3, pp. 23–24.

41. Thus P'i alters Han Yü's role as a self-appointed follower of Mencius to a sort of T'ang Confucius, whose teachings would be carried out by P'i (as Mencius transmitted Confucius's tenets).

42. Lau, *Mencius*, 7.B.4, p. 194.

43. *Literary Marsh, ch.* 7, p. 67.

44. Lau, *Mencius*, 7.B.4, pp. 194–5.

45. Lau, *Mencius*, 4.A.9, pp. 121–22.

46. This passage has not yet been located in the *Han-shu*.

47. This translation is tentative.

48. Tung Hu was a historian in the state of Chin; see Legge, *The Chinese Classics*, vol. 5, pp. 289–91. On Chao Tung see *ibid.*, "Prolegomena," pp. 45–46.

49. Li Ko was a minister to Duke Hsüan of Lu. On Chü P'u and this incident, see Wolfgang Bauer, *A Concordance to the Kuo-yü* (Taipei: Chinese Materials Research Aids Service Center, 1973), vol. 2, p. 42.

50. *Literary Marsh, ch.* 3, p. 35.

51. See Inaba, "Hi Jitsu-kyu."

52. *Literary Marsh, ch.* 2, p. 15.

Chapter Four

1. *Shih*, vol. 9, *ch.* 628, p. 7211.

2. See, for example, Liu I-sheng, *T'ang-shih hsüan-chiang* (Hong Kong: Shanghai shu-chü, 1963), pp. 156–58.

3. See "Ch'ang-ku pei-yüan hsin-sun, ssu-shou, ti-erh" in *Li Ho shih-chu* (Taipei: Shih-chieh shu-chü, 1964), p. 89.

4. Incense was used to repel lice.

5. *Wen, ch.* 771, fol. la–lb, p. 10147.

6. *Tsei*, translated here as "foible," can also mean "an insect of bane," "a plague-causing insect"; cf. Morohashi, *Daikanwa*, vol. 10, p. 11202, gloss number 36759, headnote 12.

7. *Wen*, vol. 17, *ch.* 800, fol. 13b–14a, p. 10593.

8. Wing-Tsit Chan, *The Way of Lao Tzu* (Indianapolis: Bobbs-Merrill, 1963), p. 149.

9. See Yen's biography, *Shih-chi*, vol. 7, *ch.* 67, pp. 2187–88.

10. On Liu-hsia Chih, see Watson, *Chuang tzu*, pp. 323–31.

11. Although one should not argue that only one reading of a poem is possible, there are limits imposed by convention, diction, and syntax which are sometimes exceeded in "interpretive" translations.

12. The following passage is based on Hsüeh Feng-sheng, "Elements in the Metrics of T'ang Poetry," *CYYY*, 42 (1971), pp. 467–90; Kao Yu-kung and Mei Tsu-Lin, "Syntax, Diction and Imagery in T'ang Poetry," *HJAS*, 31(1971), pp. 49–136; and Stephen Owen, "A Grammar of Court Poetry" and "Tonal Patterns" in his *Early Poetry of the T'ang* (New Haven: Yale, 1977), pp. 425–28 and 429–31.

13. *T'ang-yin kuei-chien* (Peking: Chung-hua shu-chü, 1962), *ch.* 3, pp. 13–14.

14. *Ibid.*, *ch.* 10, pp. 81–82.

15. Because of P'i's unorthodox methods of composition, there are several poems tentatively considered *p'ai-lü* here, which may in fact not properly belong to this category.

16. As can be seen in the following listing of the most prolific T'ang poets (all figures are based on the author's count and are approximate), several contemporaries of P'i, including Lu Kuei-meng, exceeded P'i's total; 1) Po Chü-i, 2931 poems; 2) Tu Fu (712–770), 1473; 3) Li Po (701–761), 1168; 4) Liu Yü-hsi (772–842), 896; 5) Yüan Chen (779–831), 843; 6) Ch'i Chi (fl. 881), 836; 7) Kuan Hsiu (832–912), 765; 8) Lu Kuei-meng, 637; 9) Li Shang-yin, 612; 10) Wang Chien (768–835), 583; 11) Wei Ying-wu (735–*ca*. 830), 579; 12) Hsieh Chou [Chiao-jan] *ca*. 734–*ca*. 800), 549; 13) Meng Chiao (751–814), 541; 14) Yao Ho (fl. 831), 536; 15) Ch'ien Ch'i (722–*ca*. 780), 533; 16) Hsü Hun (fl. 844), 533; 17) Tu Mu, 529; 18) Liu Ch'ang-ch'ing (710–*ca*. 785), 527; 19) Chang Chi (768–*ca*. 830), 511; and 20) Lo Yin, 494. Yet one should consider that much of P'i's corpus comes from a single year (870).

17. Wind (emotions) and bone (prosody) are from Section 28 of the *Wen-hsin tiao-lung*, "The Wind and the Bone"; cf. Vincent Yu-chung Shih, *The Literary Mind and the Carving of Dragons* (Taipei: Chung Hwa Book Company, 1970), pp. 227–31.

18. Hu, *T'ang-yin*, *ch.* 8, p. 66.

19. Such as Han's "Chin ts'ao, shih-shou," *Shih*, vol. 5, *ch.* 336, pp. 3760–63.

20. *Shih*, vol. 9, *ch.* 608, pp. 7012–13.

21. Chen Shih-hsiang, "The *Shih-ching*: Its Generic Significance in Chinese Literary History and Poetics," in *Studies in Chinese Literary Genres*, edited by Cyril Birch (Berkeley: University of California Press, 1974), pp. 8–41.

22. C. H. Wang, *The Bell and the Drum* (Berkeley: University of California Press, 1974), p. 112.

23. *Ch.* 7, fol. 10b *(SPPY)*. There are also parallels to the *Book of Poetry*: the comparison of the brilliance of a colt and a man in Mao 186, the

tinkling girdle gems of Mao 136, the metaphor of a lady and the brightness
of the moon in Mao 143, and the description of the royal house as a blazing
fire in Mao 10.

24. Legge, *The Chinese Classics*, vol. 3, p. 540.

25. *Shih*, vol. 9, *ch*. 608, pp. 7015–16, and *Literary Marsh*, *ch*. 10, p.
110. The *HTS* reports a series of floods and droughts for this area during the
860s, see *HTS*, vol. 3, *ch*. 35, p. 899, and *ch*. 36, pp. 935 and 940.

26. Lau, *Mencius*, 1.A.7, p. 59.

27. *Ibid*., 1.B.12, pp. 70–71; see also p. 97.

28. *Han Fei Tzu, Basic Writings* (New York: Columbia, 1964), p. 8.

29. See, for example, Liu Ta-chieh, *Chung-kuo wen-hsüeh fa-chan shih*
(Shanghai: Jen-min ch'u-pan-she, 1976), vol. 2, pp. 459–65.

30. There are several possible settings for this poem. Chang Chih-ho's
prototypical series was written near Hu-chou (see the note to the title, *Shih*,
vol. 5, *ch*. 308, p. 3491). P'i's mention of "sea perch" and "water shields"
refers to Chang Han, who abandoned a high position in the capital to return
home to the Hu-chou region after recalling the flavors of the local broth
made from water shields and of a minced dish made from sea perch (see
Chin shu, ch. 92. fol. 9a [*SPPY*]), and would seem to verify the Hu-chou
location.

31. *Shih*, vol. 9, *ch*. 613, p. 7065.

32. See his biography, *HTS*, vol. 18, *ch*. 196, pp. 5608–9.

33. See chapter 1, note 49.

34. The preface to these works is examined above in chapter 2.

35. For a discussion and translation of this series, see Nienhauser,
"Twelve Poems," in *Critical Essays*.

36. *Shih*, vol. 9, *ch*. 608, p. 7019.

37. Edwin O. Reischauer, *Ennin's Travels in T'ang China* (New York:
Ronald Press, 1955), p.110.

38. On T'ien Ch'eng-tzu (also known as Ch'en Heng), see Legge, *The
Chinese Classics*, vol. 5, p. 836; see also Teng T'o, *Hsin-pien*, p. 108, n. 12.

39. *Shih*, vol. 9, *ch*. 608, pp. 7019–20.

40. *Ibid*., pp. 7020–21.

41. *Ibid*., p. 7021.

42. Other verses in this series speak of Nan-yüeh (modern Vietnam),
Shu (Szechwan), and Hsiang-yang.

43. *Shih*, vol. 9, *ch*. 612, pp. 7061–62.

44. Chou, "P'i Jih-hsiu," p. 142.

45. *Shih*, vol. 9, *ch*. 615, p. 7093.

46. See *Shih-chi*, vol. 7, *ch*. 75, p. 2355.

47. *Shih*, vol. 9, *ch*. 615, p. 7094.

48. *Shih*, vol. 9, *ch*. 615, p. 7096.

49. *Shih-chi*, vol. 5, *ch*. 31, pp. 1468–69.

50. *Shih*, vol. 9, *ch*. 615, p. 7096.

51. *Ibid*., *ch*. 613, p. 7075.

52. Cf. Yao Ling-hsi, S*su wu hsieh hsiao-chi* [Notes on "No Evil Thoughts"] (Tientsin: Tientsin yin-shua kung-ssu, 1941), p. 165, where it is noted that deer are to be considered lascivious because the male can copulate with numerous females.

53. *Shih-shi*, vol. 10, *ch*. 118, p. 3085.

54. The "Enclosing-mists Boat" and the "Clouds-arriving Tune" both allude anachronistically to the luxuries of Emperor Wu of Han's palace, see *Tung-ming chi*, *ch*. 1, fol. 2a–2b [*Han Wei ts'ung-shu* ed.].

55. The subject of these lines is unclear.

56. *Shih*, vol. 9, *ch*. 610, p. 7039.

57. Only the title and the subject are harmonized. The rhymes and even the length of these verses vary.

58. According to the "Wu yü" chapter of the *Kuo-yü* (see Wei Chao's *Kuo-yü Wei-shih chieh* [Taipei: Shih-chieh shu-chü, n.d.], *ch*. 19, p. 448) the six-thousand-man home guard of Yüeh was made up of relatives and close associates of the king.

59. Referring to Fan Li, Kou Ch'ien's chief advisor.

60. Wu Tzu-hsü is supposedly the author of a work entitled *Shui-chan fa* [Techniques of Naval Battle]; cf. *T'ai-p'ing yü-lan*, vol. 3, *ch*. 315, fol. 2a, p. 1579.

61. Feng I, sometimes called Feng Hsün or Ho Po, was the god of the seas and rivers.

62. *Shih*, vol. 9, *ch*. 618, p. 7122.

63. *Shih-chi*, vol. 5, *ch*. 31, p. 1469.

64. *Ibid.*, p. 1468.

65. "Gold grease" *(chin-kao)* is a type of immortality drug; see J. D. Frodsham, *The Murmuring Stream* (Kuala Lumpur: University of Malaysia Press, 1967), vol. 2, p. 182, n. 17, where "the fat of gold [*chin-kao*]" is said to be the second (to cinnabar) most effective of these elixirs.

66. See *P'ei-wen yün-fu* (Taipei: Shang-wu yin-shu-kuan, 1974), vol. 5, p. 4236.b, and Yang Hsiung, *Fang-yen chien-shu* (Taipei: Wen-hai ch'u-pan-she, 1967), *ch*. 9, fol. 10b, p. 308, respectively.

67. *Shih*, vol. 9, *ch*. 611, p. 7055.

68. Line 3, although not supportive of this interpretation, echoes Tu Fu's "Autumn Meditations, number eight"; cf. the translation by Kao and Mei, "Syntax," p. 80. On the symbolism of the pomegranate, see also Bo Gyllensvärd, "A Botanical Excursion in the Kempe Collection," *BMFEA*, 37 (1965), p. 171; James J. Y. Liu, poems 15–16 and 17–18 in *Li Shang-yin. Ninth-Century Baroque Chinese Poet* (Chicago: University of Chicago Press, 1969), pp. 82–84; "Yu tseng Shih-niang," a poem from the erotic novella, *Yu hsien-k'u*, in *Ch'üan T'ang shih i*, *ch*. C, in *Shih*, vol. 12, p. 10218; a love poem by the infamous Empress Wu of the T'ang, "Ju-i niang," in *Shih*, vol. 1, *ch*. 5, pp. 58–59; and finally, an erotic passage comparing the undulations of the vagina to pomegranate seeds, see *Ch'un-meng so-yen* (Trifling Tale of a Spring Dream), published privately by R.H. van Gulik

(Tokyo, 1950), p. 17, and Jordan D. Paper's unpublished translation (available from the library of the Institute for Sex Research, Indiana University), p. 19.

69. *Shih*, vol. 2, *ch*. 143, p. 1448.

70. Cf. Schafer, *The Divine Woman* (Berkeley: University of California Press, 1973), pp. 38–42.

71. *Shih*, vol. 9, *ch*. 613, p. 7071. As incongruous as it may seem, this poem is erotic. Although this sort of explication lies beyond the scope of the present study, the reader is referred to R. H. van Gulik, *Sexual Life in Ancient China* (Leiden: Brill, 1961), p. 201, n. 1, and to my "Diction, Dictionaries, and the Translation of Classical Chinese Poetry," *TP*, 64 (1978) pp. 30–50.

72. Red is one of P'i's favorite colors (along with purple). It occurs once every 397 characters in his recent-style poetry, and once every 1873 in his old-style verse. As a means of comparison, Maureen Robertson has found that Tu Fu uses red on a mean rate of 1:1364; Li Po, 1:1222; Han Yü, 1:1075; and Li Ho, 1:333 (see her "Poetic Diction in the Works of Li He (891–917)" [unpublished Ph.D. dissertation, University of Washington, 1970], p. 87). See also Schafer, *Vermilion Bird*, p. 259.

73. P'i may be suggesting that Lu send him a cassia branch in return, since already in the T'ang "to break off a branch of cassia" meant to pass the examinations, and since P'i had previously exhorted Lu to take the examinations; see Chou, "P'i Jih-hsiu," p. 121.

74. *Shih*, vol. 9, *ch*. 613, p. 7072.

75. On Han Yen, see his biographies in *Shih-chi*, vol. 10, *ch*. 125, pp. 3194–95, and *Han-shu*, vol. 11, *ch*. 93, pp. 3724–25. On his habit of shooting golden pellets, see *Hsi-ching tsa-chi*, *ch*. 4, fol. 2b–3a *(SPTK)*.

76. *Mu T'ien-tzu chuan*, *ch*. 1, fol. 2a *(SPTK)*.

77. See Chao Hsüeh-min, *Pen-ts'ao kang-mu shih-i* (Hong Kong: Shang-wu yin-shu-kuan, 1971), p. 312.

78. *Shih*, vol. 9, *ch*. 615, p. 7095.

79. In his *Poems of the Late T'ang* (Baltimore: Penguin, 1965), pp. 36–37.

80. See *A Concordance to Tu Fu*, vol. 2, p. 369.

81. *Shih*, vol. 9, *ch*. 613, p. 7070.

82. New Haven: Far Eastern Publications, Yale University, 1966.

83. Mao number 57; Karlgren, p. 38.

84. The expression *t'ien-nü*, "Heavenly Daughters," may refer as well to the Weaving Girl.

85. *Shih*, vol. 9, *ch*. 615, p. 7099. The translation is based upon that of Edward H. Schafer, *The Vermilion Bird* (Berkeley: University of California Press, 1967), p. 203.

86. Schafer, *Vermilion*, p. 203.

87. Waley, *Analects*, p. 147.

88. En-wang Palace, or the Palace of the Prince of En, was the resi-

dence of the sixth son of Emperor Tai, Li Lien (d. 817). Exactly what Hsü's connection with this royal person and his palace was remains unclear. See also *CTS*, vol. 10, *ch*. 116, p. 3392.

89. *Shih*, vol. 9, *ch*. 609, pp. 7028–29.

90. Miao, "P'i Jih-hsiu," p. 387.

91. *Shih*, vol. 9, *ch*. 611, p. 7048.

92. Peking: Chung-hua shu-chü, 1958, p. 61.

93. *Shih*, vol. 9, *ch*. 611, p. 7047.

94. HIUAEN TEU THING SHAENG NGEI.

95. Cf. "Preface to the *Poetry in Miscellaneous Forms*," in chapter 2.

96. See "Preface to the *Poetry in Miscellaneous Forms*," *Shih*, vol. 9, *ch*. 616, p. 7102, and note 95.

97. Although there are lichens which are red in color, this line is puzzling since *hsien*, "lichen," is usually depicted as green in Chinese poetry.

98. *Shih*, vol. 9, *ch*. 616, p. 7102.

99. Tonal pattern is as follows (X–uneven, O–even):

OO XX OO X/XX OO XX O/OX XO OX X/XO OX XO O
OO XX OO X/XX OO XX O/OX XO OX X/XO OX XO O.

100. *Shih*, vol. 9, *ch*. 616, p. 7104.

101. *Ibid.*

102. Chang harmonized a number of poems with P'i; see his corpus and biographical note in *Shih*, vol. 10, *ch*. 631, pp. 7235–37, and *T'ang-shih chi-shih*, vol. 2, *ch*. 64, p. 961.

103. *Shih*, vol. 11, *ch*. 793, pp. 8928–29.

104. See Schafer's "The Sky River," *JAOS*, 94 (1974), pp. 404–5.

105. See *T'ai-p'ing yü-lan*, vol. 1, *ch*. 8, fol. 11a, p. 171, and Schafer, "Sky River," p. 405.

106. The "amber-jade branch" alludes to the "Li sao"; see *Ch'ü Yüan fu chiao-chu*, edited by Chiang Liang-fu (Hong Kong: Chung-hua shu-chü, 1972), *ch*. 1, p. 93.

Chapter Five

1. *Ch*. 2, p. 7.

2. Vol. 5, *ch*. 60, p. 1608.

3. *HTS*, vol. 5, *ch*. 59, p. 1564, for example, records a *Lu-men chia-ch'ao* in ninety *chüan*.

4. Shanghai: Tung-fang shu-chü, 1934, *ch*. 18, pp. 192–93.

5. See Hsiao, "Ch'ien yen," p. 5, and note 31 to chapter 1 above.

6. *Ibid.*

7. See his *Jung-chai sui-pi wu chi* (Taipei: Shang-wu yin-shu-kuan, 1956), vol. 3, *ch*. 16, fol. 2b and fol. 15a.

8. *Ch*. 8, p. 144.

9. See Hu Yü-chin, *Ssu-k'u ch'üan-shu tsung-mu t'i-yao pu-cheng*,

edited by Wang Hsin-fu (Shanghai: Chung-hua shu-chü, 1964), vol. 2, *ch*. 44, p. 1220, and *Tseng-ting ssu-k'u chien-mu piao-chu*, compiled by Shao I-ch'en (1810–1861) (Shanghai: Chung-hua shu-chü, 1959), p. 674. The version upon which the *SPTK* edition is based was printed about 1520 and a small-character edition was produced at about the same time.

10. Entitled *T'ang P'i Ts'ung-shih ch'ang-ch'ou shih*; see Hu Yü-chin, *ibid*.

11. See the nine works included in *chüan* 26 *(Wei-yüan shan-t'ang Woodblock* ed.).

12. Lu Hsün [Chou Shu-jen], "Hsiao-p'in-wen te wei-chi," in *Lu Hsün ch'üan-chi* (Peking: Jen-min wen-hsüeh ch'u-pan-she, 1973), vol. 5, p. 171.

13. See, for example, *Ch'üan T'ang shih ching-hua*, edited by Liu Ya-tzu and Liu Wu-chi (Reprint; Hong Kong: Wen-yüan shu-tien, n.d.), pp. 256–58.

14. See Ku's *Chung-kuo wen-hsüeh-shih ta-kang* (Shanghai: Commercial Press, 1926), p. 207; Hu's *Chung-kuo wen-hsüeh-shih* (Shanghai: Pei-hsin shu-chü, 1932), p. 143; and T'an's *Chung-kuo wen-hsüeh-shih* (Shanghai: Kuang-ming shu-chu, 1935), p. 208.

15. Vol. 1 (Shanghai: Commercial Press, 1935), pp. 284–85.

16. *Wen I-to ch'üan-chi* (Shanghai: K'ai-ming shu-tien, 1948), vol. 4, pp. 429–31.

17. See articles by Miao Yüeh (2) and Hsiao Ti-fei, pp. 371–411.

18. See the obverse side of the title page, 1965 reprint.

19. See pp. 43, 61, 107–9.

20. Pp. 459–60.

21. *Shih*, vol. 7, *ch*. 426, p. 4689.

22. See Selected Bibliography, section 3 of the Primary Sources.

23. Cf. pp. 259–66.

24. Wellek and Austin Warren, *Theory of Literature* (New York: Harcourt, Brace and World, 1956), p. 248.

Selected Bibliography

PRIMARY SOURCES

1. Chinese Editions

HSIAO TI-FEI, editor. *P'i-tzu wen-sou* [Literary Marsh of Master P'i]. Peking: Chung-hua shu-chü, 1959. A punctuated and collated version of the standard collection of P'i's works. This corpus includes thirty-six old-style poems and all but seven of his prose pieces; it represents his creative production prior to 867.

P'i-tzu wen-sou. [*SPTK* ed.].

Sung-ling chi [Pine Knoll Anthology]. [*Hu-pei hsien-sheng i-shu* ed.]. A collection of the approximately seven hundred poems written during 870 by the Soochow literary coterie to which P'i belonged, including over three hundred poems by P'i. Most are works harmonized with Lu Kuei-meng.

TS'AO YIN (1658–1712), compiler. *Ch'üan T'ang-shih* (Complete T'ang Poetry). 12 vols. Taipei: Ming-lun ch'u-pan-she, 1971. P'i's 405 old- and new-style poems are included in vol. 9, *ch.* 608–16, pp. 7012–107. His linked-verse (eight poems) is found in vol. 11, *ch.* 793, pp. 8927–30. There are no poems by P'i included in any of the works designed to supplement the *Ch'üan T'ang-shih.*

TUNG KAO (1740–1818), compiler. *Ch'üan T'ang-wen* (Complete T'ang Prose). 20 vols. Taipei: Wen-yu shu-tien, 1972. P'i's 101 pieces of prose and prose-poetry are to be found in vol. 17. *ch.* 796–99, pp. 10523–84.

2. Other Annotated Sources

CHANG CH'I-WEN. *T'ang-tai san-wen hsüan-chu* [Annotated Selections of T'ang Dynasty Prose]. Peking: Chung-hua shu-chü, 1977. Contains annotated versions of two pieces of P'i's prose (pp. 169–72).

CHU TUNG-JUN. *Chung-kuo li-tai wen-hsüeh tso-p'in hsüan.* Hong Kong: Wen-hsüeh yen-chiu-she, n.d. One poem and two pieces of prose are annotated (vol. 2A, pp. 329–30 and 483–84, respectively).

KAO MING. *Sui T'ang Wu-tai wen-hui* [A Collection of the Prose from the Sui, T'ang and Five Dynasty Periods]. Hong Kong: Chung-hua ts'ung-

shu wei-yüan-hui, 1957. Punctuated versions of nine prose pieces and
one prose-poem, including the complete text of the *Lu-men yin-shu*.

PEI-CHING TA-HSÜEH CHUNG-WEN-HSI WEN-HSÜEH YEN-CHIU-SHENG
TZU-LIAO TSU [Source Material Group of the Graduate Students in
Literature in the Chinese Department, Peking University], editors.
Chung-kuo li-tai nung-min wen-t'i wen-hsüeh tzu-liao [Literary Source
Material on Peasant Problems throughout Chinese History]. Peking:
Chung-hua shu-chü, 1959. Contains six poems (pp. 48–49).

SHEN PING. *T'ang Sung san-wen hsüan-chu* [Annotated Selection of T'ang
Dynasty Prose]. Taipei: Cheng-chung shu-chü, 1969. Annotated version of one prose piece (pp. 126–27).

TENG T'O. *Hsin-pien T'ang-shih san-pai shou* [A Newly Compiled Three
Hundred Poems of the T'ang]. Peking: Chung-hua shu-chü, 1958. Contains seven poems with annotations (pp. 43, 61, 107–9).

3. Western-language Translations

LIU WU-CHI and IRVING YUCHENG LO. *Sunflower Splendor*. New York:
Doubleday/Anchor Press, 1975. Contains translations of eight poems
by P'i Jih-hsiu, pp. 259–66.

SCHAFER, EDWARD H. *Golden Peaches of Samarkand*. Berkeley: University of California Press, 1963. Contains translations of three of P'i's
poems on pp. 99, 123, and 129. See also pp. 253, 271.

––––––. *Vermilion Bird*. Berkeley: University of California Press, 1967.
Contains a single translation, p. 89. See also p. 204.

SECONDARY SOURCES

1. Biographical and Critical Articles

CHOU LIEN-K'UAN. "P'i Jih-hsiu te sheng-p'ing chi ch'i tso-p'in [P'i Jih-
hsiu's Life and Works], *Ling-nan hsüeh-pao*, 12.1 (June 1952), pp.
113–44. The most complete and most reliable introduction to P'i Jih-
hsiu.

FU-TAN TA-HSÜEH CHUNG-WEN-HSI CHUNG-KUO WEN-HSÜEH P'I-PING-
SHIH SUI-T'ANG-WU-TAI HSIAO-TSU [History of Chinese Literary
Criticism of Aurora University: Sui, T'ang, Five Dynasties Group]. "Tu
Mu, P'i Jih-hsiu te wen-hsüeh p'i-p'an" [Literary Criticism of Tu Mu
and P'i Jih-hsiu], *Wen-hsüeh i-ch'an*, p. 4, in *Kuang-ming jih-pao*,
September 11, 1960. P'i Jih-hsiu's emphasis on the socio-political content and use of literature is praised. His appreciation of "romantic"
poets such as Li Po and Li Ho is noted. His "formalist" and Confucian
writings are then briefly condemned. Discussion of P'i follows a separate evaluation of Tu Mu. No attempt at a comparative evaluation is
made.

FUKUMOTO MASAICHI. "Hi Jitsu-kyu o megutte, I, II" [Concerning P'i
Jih-hsiu, I, II], *Daian*, 11.8 (August 1965) and 11.9 (September 1965),
pp. 23–26 and 23–25, respectively. Two brief notices of P'i's life and

works. Literary life is divided into two eras: Soochow, for which he has traditionally been acclaimed, and earlier didactic work, which is the source of recent critical interest.

HSIAO TI-FEI. "Chiao-tien P'i-tzu wen-sou shuo-ming—chien lun yu-kuan P'i Jih-hsiu chu wen-t'i" [Some Explanatory Comments on the Collated and Punctuated Editions of the *Literary Marsh of Master P'i* with Several Questions Concerning P'i Jih-hsiu], *Wen-shih-che,* January 1958, pp. 3707–13.

————. "Ch'ien-yen" [Introduction]. *P'i-tzu wen-sou.* Peking: Chung-hua shu-chü, 1959, pp. 1–21. Argues that the *Literary Marsh* is more than just a preexamination collection—it is a literary work in the school of realism such as is found in the *Book of Poetry.* Traces textual history and discusses some biographical problems.

————. "Lun yu-kuan P'i Jih-hsiu chu wen-t'i" [On Some Questions concerning P'i Jih-hsiu], in *T'ang-shih yen-chiu lun-wen-chi* [hereafter cited as *T'ang-shih*], edited by the Editorial Section of the Peoples' Literature Publishing House. Peking: Jen-min wen-hsüeh ch'u-pan-she, 1959, pp. 402–11. Believes 1) that P'i was born 834–38, 2) that he served Huang Ch'ao, and 3) that he was executed by T'ang after Huang Ch'ao's defeat.

INABA ICHIRŌ. "Hi Jitsu-kyu oyobi Tan-Chō-Riku shi no *Shunjū* kenkyū" [Studies of the *Spring and Autumn Annals* by P'i Jih-hsiu and Messrs. Tan (Chu), Chao (Kuang), and Lu (Ch'un)], in Utsunomiya Kiyoyoshi, ed. *Chūgoku chūseishi kenkyū—Rikuchō Sui Tō no shakai to bunka* (A Study of Chinese Medieval History—The Society and Culture of the Six Dynasties, Sui and T'ang). Tokyo: Tokai University Press, 1970, pp. 389–97. Traces the critical spirit of P'i's study of the *Spring and Autumn Annals* to Liu Chih-chi. Argues that this spirit was transmitted by Tan Chü, Chao Kuang, and Lu Ch'un, and that their major contribution was in rejecting the three traditional commentaries to this work.

MASUDA KIYOHIDE. "Hi Jitsu-kyu no seigakufu" [P'i Jih-hsiu's "Orthodox Music Bureau Poems"]. *Shinagaku Kenkyū,* 24/25 (1959), pp. 163–71. Gives historical background of P'i's life. Traces influence of Yüan Chieh's literary *yüeh-fu* on P'i. Discusses P'i's "Orthodox Music Bureau Poems" and argues the importance that this genre held for P'i's critical thought.

————. "Tō no Hi Jitsu-kyu no 'Seigakufu' to jiji hihan" [P'i Jih-hsiu's "Orthodox Music Bureau Poems" and Criticism of Current Affairs], in *Gakufu no rekishiteki kenkyū* (A Historical Study of *Yüeh-fu*). Tokyo: Sōbunsha, 1975, pp. 407–30. Notes P'i's volatile temper and the influence of Yüan Chieh. Presents short exegeses of this series of poems; concludes that although P'i followed earlier poets in form, the social criticism of his poems was more incisive than that of his predecessors.

MIAO YÜEH. "P'i Jih-hsiu te shih-chi ssu-hsiang chi ch'i tso-p'in" [Bio-graphical Facts, Thought and Works of P'i Jih-hsiu], in T'ang-shih, pp. 371–89. Good introduction to Pi's life. Where Miao disagrees with Chou Lien-k'uan, however, Chou's interpretations seem to be prefer-able. Describes two schools of late T'ang poetry: one following Po Chü-i was socially concerned; the other, modeled on Han Yü, sought to shock the reader by obscurity or ambiguity. P'i was influenced by both schools.

―――. "Tsai-lun P'i Jih-hsiu ts'an-chia Huang Ch'ao ch'i-i-chün te wen-t'i" [Once Again the Question of P'i Jih-hsiu's Participation in Huang Ch'ao's Insurrectionary Army], in T'ang-shih, pp. 390–401. Argues against the theory that P'i came from peasant origins; throws further doubt on the theory that he participated in Huang Ch'ao's rebellion.

NAKAJIMA CHŌBUN. "Hi Jitsu-kyu." In Tōdai no shijin—sono denki [The T'ang Poets—Their Biographies], edited by Ogawa Tamaki. Tokyo: Taishūkan shoten, 1975, pp. 581–89. Contains a carefully annotated version of the biographical notice for P'i Jih-hsiu in the T'ang ts'ai-tzu chuan, a translation, and an excellent bibliography.

OGAWA SHŌICHI. "Hi Jitsu-kyu ni tsuite" [On P'i Jih-hsiu], in Zen Tōshi zakki [Miscellaneous Notes on the Complete T'ang Poems]. Kyoto: Ibundo shoten, 1969, pp. 78–109. Good introduction to P'i Jih-hsiu. Adds the idea of P'i's unrestrained character as an explanation for his actions. Also gives impressive supplementary material on background of this period. Good bibliographic discussion. Long passages on his appreciation of Mencius and his didactic criticism and verse.

2. Works on the T'ang Dynasty or T'ang Literature

BALAZS, ETIENNE. "Beiträge zur Wirtschaftsgeschichte der T'ang-Zeit," Mitteilungen des Seminars für orientalische Sprachen, 24(1931), pp. 1–92; 25(1932), pp. 1–73; 26(1933), pp. 1–62.

CH'EN HUNG-CH'IH. Ch'üan T'ang-wen chi-shih. 3 vols. Peking: Chung-hua shu-chü, 1959.

CH'EN, KENNETH. "The Economic Background of the Hui-ch'ang Suppres-sion of Buddhism," HJAS, 19(1956), pp. 67–105.

CHI YU-KUNG (fl. 1135). T'ang shih chi-shih. 2 vols. Taipei: Chung-hua shu-chü, 1959.

CH'IEN I. Nan-pu hsin-shu (Ao-ya-t'ang ts'ung shu ed.).

CH'IEN MU. "Tso-lun T'ang-tai ku-wen yün-tung" [Notes on the Ku-wen Movement of the T'ang Period], Hsin-ya hsüeh-pao, 3(1958), pp. 35–44.

CHOU PAO-CHU. "T'ang-mo nung-min chan-cheng-shih chung i-ko wen-t'i ti shang-chüeh" [A Discussion of a Problem in the History of Peasant Warfare in the Late T'ang], Shixue yuekan, 1956.6(June, 1959), pp. 37–39.

CHOU TSU-CHUAN. Sui T'ang Wu-tai wen-hsüeh shih [A Literary History of

Sui, T'ang and the Five Dynasties]. Foochow: Fu-chien jen-min ch'u-pan-she, 1958.

EIDE, ELLING O. "On Li Po," in *Perspectives*, pp. 367–403.

FORKE, ALFRED. "Die T'ang Zeit," in *Geschichte der mittelalterlichen chinesischen Philosophie*. Hamburg: Cram, DeGruyter and Company, 1964, pp. 283–371.

FRANKEL, HANS H. "The Contemplation of the Past in T'ang Poetry," in *Perspectives*, pp. 345–65.

_____. "T'ang Literati: A Composite Biography," in Arthur F. Wright and Denis Twitchett, eds. *Confucian Personalities*. Stanford: Stanford University Press, 1962, pp. 65–83.

GERNET, JACQUES. *Les aspects économiques du bouddhisme dans la societe chinoise du Ve au Xe siécle*. Saigon: Publications de l'Ecole Française d'Extreme-orient, 1956.

GILES, LIONEL. "The Lament of the Lady of Ch'in," *TP*, 24(1926), pp. 305–80.

GRAHAM, A. C. *Poems of the Late T'ang*. Baltimore: Penguin, 1965.

HANABUSA HIDEKI. *Han Yu kanshi sakuhin* (A Concordance to the Poems of Han Yü). Kyoto: Kyoto furitsu daigaku jimbun gakkai, 1954.

HARTMAN, CHARLES. "Language and Allusion in the Poetry of Han Yü— the Autumn Sentiments." (Unpublished Ph.D. dissertation, Indiana University, 1974).

HSÜ SUNG (1781–1848), compiler. *T'ang liang-ching ch'eng-fang k'ao*. Taipei: I-wen yin-shu-kuan, 1967.

_____. *Teng-k'o-chi k'ao*. 3 vols. Taipei: Ching-sheng wen-wu kung-ying kung-ssu, 1972.

HSÜ, VIVIAN. "The Element of Tone in the Prosody of T'ang Poetry," *JOS*, 11.2(July, 1973), pp. 220–26.

HSÜ, WEN-YÜ. "Wan-T'ang-shih chih chu-liu" [The Major Currents of Late T'ang Poetry], *Wen-shih-che*, 1959.9, pp. 10–14.

HSÜEH, FENG-SHENG. "Elements in the Metrics of T'ang Poetics," *CYYY*, 42(1941), pp. 467–90.

HU CHEN-HENG (1569–1644/45). *T'ang yin kuei-ch'ien*. Peking: Chung-hua shu-chü, 1959.

HUANG CH'ING-SHIH. "Li Shang-yin yü Ling-hu Fu-tzu" [Li Shang-yin and the Ling-hus, Father and Son], in *T'ang-shih*, pp. 353–59.

IRICK, ROBERT L., compiler. *A Concordance to the Poems of Li Ho (790–816)*. Taipei: Chinese Materials and Research Aids Service Center, 1963.

JAKOBSON, ROMAN. "Le Dessin Prosodique ou le principe modulaire dans le vers réguliér chinois," *Change*, 2(1969), pp. 39–48.

JOHNSON, DAVID. "The Last Years of a Great Clan: The Li Family of Chao Chün in the Late T'ang and Early Sung," *HJAS*, 37(1977), pp. 5–102.

KANO NAOKI. "Tōshidai no Keigaku" [Classical Studies of the T'ang

Period], Chūgoku tetsugaku shi. 6th reprint; Tokyo: Iwanami shotien, 1965, pp. 336–49.

KAO PU-YING. T'ang Sung shih chü-yao. 3 vols. Peking: Chung-hua shu-chü, 1963.

KAO YU-KUNG and MEI TSU-LIN. "Syntax, Diction and Imagery in T'ang Poetry," HJAS, 31(1971), pp. 49–136.

LATTIMORE, DAVID. "Allusion and T'ang Poetry," Perspectives, pp. 405–39.

LEVY, HOWARD S. "An Historical Introduction of the Events which Culminated in the Huang Ch'ao Rebellion," Phi Theta Annual, 2(1951), pp. 79–103.

————. Biography of Huang Ch'ao. Berkeley and Los Angeles: University of California Press, 1955.

LIU HSÜ (887–946), compiler. Chiu T'ang-shu (Old T'ang History). 16 vols. Peking: Chung-hua shu-chü, 1975.

LIU, JAMES J. Y. "Ambiguities in Li Shang-yin's Poetry," in Wen-lin, edited by Tse-tsung Chow. Madison, Milwaukee, and London: University of Wisconsin Press, 1968, pp. 65–84.

————. Chinese Theories of Literature. Chicago: University of Chicago Press, 1975.

————. The Poetry of Li Shang-yin, Ninth-century Baroque Chinese Poet. Chicago: University of Chicago Press, 1969.

LIU, JEN-KAI. Die boshaften, unbotmässigen und rebellischen Beamten in der Neuen Offiziellen Dynastiegeschichte der T'ang. Hamburg: Gesellschaft für Natur- und Völkerkunde Ostasiens, 1976.

LIU, MAU-TSAI. "Das Bild in der Dichtung der T'ang Zeit," OE, 16(1969), pp. 181–208.

LO HSIANG-LIN. T'ang-tai wen-hua shih [A History of T'ang Culture]. Taipei: Shang-wu yin-shu-kuan, 1968.

LO KEN-TSE. Wan-T'ang Wu-tai wen-hsüeh p'i-p'ing-shih [A History of Literary Criticism in the Late T'ang and Five Dynasties]. Shanghai: Commercial Press, 1945.

LÜ HSIN-YUAN, compiler. T'ang wen shih-i. Taipei: Wen-hai shu-chü, 1962.

LÜ SSU-MIEN. Sui-t'ang Wu-tai shih [A History of Sui, T'ang and Five Dynasties]. 2 vols. Shanghai: Chung-hua shu-chü, 1959.

MA, Y. W. "Han Yü and Ch'uan-ch'i Literature," JOS, 7(1969), pp. 195–223.

McLEOD, RUSSELL. "The Baroque as a Period Concept in Chinese Literature," Tamkang Review, 7.2(October 1976), pp. 185–211.

McMULLEN, DAVID. "Historical and Literary Theory in the Mid-Eighth Century," in Perspectives, pp. 307–42.

MAENO NAOAKI, editor. Tōshi kanshō jiten (Dictionary for Appreciating T'ang Poetry). Tokyo: Tokyodōshuppan, 1970.

MEKADA MAKOTO. "Chu-ban Tō no shiron to Sikū To no 'Nijishi shihin' " (The Theory of Poetry in the Middle and Late T'ang Period and the "Erh-shih-ssu shih-p'in" by Ssu-k'ung T'u), *Chūgoku Koten Kenkyū*, 20(1975), pp. 62–73.

NABA TOSHISADA. *Tōdai shakai bunka shi kenkyū* (Historical Studies on the Society and Culture of T'ang China). Tokyo: Sōfunsha, 1974.

NIEH I-CHUNG. *Nieh I-chung shih; Tu Hsün-ho shih*. Peking: Chung-hua shu-chü, 1959.

NIENHAUSER, WILLIAM H., JR. " 'Twelve Poems Propagating the Music Bureau Ballad': Yüan Chieh's (719–772) *Hsi yüeh-fu shih-erh shou*," in *Critical Essays on Chinese Literature*. Hong Kong: Chinese University of Hong Kong Press, 1976, pp. 135–47.

OTAGI HAJIME. "Todai kohan ni okeru shakai henshitsu no ikkōsatsu" (A Study of Social Change in the Latter Half of the T'ang), *Tōho gakuhō*, 42(March 1971), pp. 91–126.

OWEN, STEPHEN. *The Poetry of Meng Chiao and Han Yü*. New Haven: Yale University Press, 1975.

————. *Poetry of the Early T'ang*. London and New Haven: Yale University Press, 1977.

PERRY, JOHN CURTIS and BARDWELL L. SMITH. *Essays on T'ang Society, The Interplay of Social, Political and Economic Forces*. Leiden: E. J. Brill, 1976.

PETERSON, CHARLES. "Regional Defense against the Central Power: The Huai-hsi Campaign, 815–817," in Frank A. Kierman, Jr. and John K. Fairbank, editors, *Chinese Ways in Warfare*. Cambridge, Mass.: Harvard University Press, 1974, pp. 123–50.

PULLEYBLANK, E. G. "Liu K'o, A Forgotten Rival of Han Yü," *Asia Major, New Series*, 7(1959), pp. 145–60.

————. "Neo-Confucianism and Neo-Legalism in T'ang Intellectual Life, 755–806," in *Confucian Persuasion*, Arthur F. Wright, ed. Stanford: Stanford University Press, 1960, pp. 77–114.

REISCHAUER, EDWIN O. "Notes on T'ang Dynasty Sea Routes," *HJAS*, 5(1940–41), pp. 142–64.

————. *Ennin's Diary: The Record of a Pilgrim to T'ang in Search of the Law*. New York: Ronald Press, 1955.

ROBERTSON, MAUREEN A. " '. . . To Convey what is Precious': Ssu-K'ung T'u's Poetics and the 'Erh-shih-ssu Shih-P'in' " in *Transition and Permanence: Chinese History and Culture*, David C. Buxbaum and Frederick W. Mote, eds. Hong Kong: Cathay Press, 1972, pp. 323–57.

DES ROTOURS, ROBERT. "La revolte de P'ang Hiun," *TP*, 56(1970), pp. 229–40.

————. "Le *T'ang Lieou Tien*, décrit-il exactement les institutions en usage sous la dynastie des T'ang?" *Journal asiatique*, 263(1975), pp. 185–201.

————. *Traité des examens*. Paris: Leroux, 1932.

————. *Traité des fonctionnaires et traité de l'armée.* 2 vols. Leiden: E. J. Brill, 1947–48.

SCHAFER, EDWARD H. *First Supplement to Mathews.* Berkeley: Department of Oriental Languages, 1973.

————. "Li Te-yü and the Azalea," *Etudes Asiatiques,* 18–19 (1965), pp. 105–14.

————. "Mineral Imagery in the Paradise Poems of Kuan-hsiu," *Asia Major, New Series,* 10(1963), pp. 73–102.

————. *Pacing the Void, T'ang Approaches to the Stars.* Berkeley: University of California Press, 1977.

————. "Preliminary Remarks on the Structure and Imagery of 'Classical Chinese' Language of the Medieval Period," *TP,* 50 (1963), pp. 257–64.

————. *The Golden Peaches of Samarkand.* Berkeley: University of California Press, 1963.

————. "The Last Years of Ch'ang-an," *OE,* 10(1963), pp. 133–79.

————. *The Vermilion Bird.* Berkeley: University of California Press, 1967.

SCHMIDT, JERRY D. "Han Yü and his Ku-shih Poetry."(Unpublished M.A. thesis, University of British Columbia, 1969).

SHEN PING. *T'ang Sung san-wen hsüan.* Taipei: Cheng-chung shu-chü, 1969.

SOMERS, ROBERT MILTON. "The Collapse of the T'ang Order." (Unpublished Ph.D. dissertation, Yale University, 1975).

SOUTH, MARGARET TUDOR. "Li Ho and the New Yüeh-fu Movement," *Journal of the Oriental Society of Australia,* 4(1966), pp. 49–61.

————. *Li Ho, A Scholar-official of the Yuan-ho Period (806–821).* Adelaide: Libraries of South Australia, 1967.

STIMSON, HUGH M. *Fifty-five T'ang Poems.* New Haven: Far Eastern Publications, Yale University, 1976.

————. *T'ang Poetic Vocabulary.* New Haven: Far Eastern Publications, Yale University, 1976.

————. *The Jongyuan In Yunn.* New Haven: Far Eastern Publications, Yale University, 1966.

SUNG CH'I (998–1061) and OU-YANG HSIU (1007–1072), compilers. *Hsin T'ang-shu* (New T'ang History). 20 vols. Peking: Chung-hua shu-chü, 1975.

SUNG MIN-CH'IU (1019–1079), compiler. *T'ang-tai chao-ling chi.* Commercial Press, 1959.

TAN, MABEL. "Conformity and Originality in the Poetry of Tu Mu (803–852)," *Literature East and West,* 15(1971), pp. 244–59.

T'AN (née LI) TSUNG-MU. *Tu Mu yen-chiu tzu-liao hui-pien.* Taipei: I-wen yin-shu kuan, 1972.

T'ANG CH'ENG-YEH. *Li Te-yü yen-chiu.* Taipei: Hsüeh-sheng shu-chü, 1974.

T'ang-jen hsüan T'ang-shih. Hong Kong: Chung-hua shu-chü, n.d.

TOYODA JŌ. *Tōshi kenkyū.* Tokyo: Yōtoku sha, 1948. Has a useful appendix on colloquialisms of T'ang Poetry, pp. 187–258.

TS'EN CHUNG-MEN. *Sui-T'ang shih.* Peking: Kao-teng chiao-yü ch'u-pan-she, 1957.

TWITCHETT, DENIS. "Chinese Social History from the Seventh to Tenth Centuries," *Past and Present,* 35(December 1966), pp. 28–53.

———. *Financial Administration under the T'ang Dynasty.* Cambridge: Cambridge University Press, 1963.

———. *Land Tenure and Social Order in T'ang and Sung China.* London: School of Oriental and African Studies, 1962.

———. "Merchant, Trade and Government in Late T'ang," *Asia Major, New Series,* 14(1968), pp. 63–95.

———. "Provincial Autonomy and Central Finance in Late T'ang," *Asia Major, New Series,* 11(1965), pp. 211–32.

WALEY, ARTHUR. *The Life and Times of Po Chü-i.* London: George Allen and Unwin, Ltd., 1951.

———. *The Real Tripitaka and Other Pieces.* London: George Allen and Unwin, Ltd., 1952.

WANG CH'IN-JO (fl. 1010), compiler. *Ts'e-fu yüan-kuei.* Taipei: Ch'ing-hua shu-chü, 1967.

WANG GUNGWU. "The Middle Yangtze in T'ang Politics," *Perspectives,* pp. 193–253.

WANG KUO-YÜAN, compiler. *T'ang-jen ch'uan-ch'i hsiao-shuo.* Taipei: Shih-chieh shu-chü, 1959.

WANG P'U (923–982), compiler. *T'ang hui-yao.* Peking: Chung-hua shu-chü, 1955.

WANG TE-CHEN, editor. *Lo Yin nien-p'u.* Shanghai: Commercial Press, 1937.

WANG TING-PAO. *T'ang chih-yen.* Shanghai: Chung-hua shu-chü, 1959.

WENG TA-TS'AO. *Huang Ch'ao lun.* Shanghai: Commercial Press, 1950.

WRIGHT, ARTHUR F. and DENIS C. TWITCHETT, editors. *Perspectives on the T'ang.* New Haven: Yale University Press, 1973.

WU T'ING-HSIEH. *T'ang fang-chen nien-piao* in *Erh-shih-wu shih pu-pien.* Taipei: K'ai-ming shu-tien, 1967, vol. 6, pp. 7283–570.

YAMAUCHI HARUO. *To Baku shi sakuin* (An Index to Tu Mu's Poetical Works). Kyoto: Ibundo, 1972.

YANG CHIH-MEI. "Huang Ch'ao ta ch'i-i" [Huang Ch'ao's Great Insurrection], in *Chung-kuo nung-min ch'i-i lun-chi.* Peking: Wu-shih nien-tai ch'u-pan-she, 1954, pp. 143–53.

YANG CHUNG-I. "Lower Castes in the T'ang Dynasty," in E-tu Zen Sun and John de Francis, editors. *Chinese Social History: Translations of Selected Studies.* Washington: American Council of Learned Societies, 1956, pp. 185–91.

YANG TSUNG-SHIH, editor. *Hsiang-yang hsien-chih*. Taipei: Taiwan hsüeh-sheng shu-chü, 1965.

YOSHIMINE NORIO. "Kō Sō no ran" [Huang Ch'ao's Revolt], in *Tōyōshi kenkyū*, 14.4(March 1956), pp. 71–92.

YU MOU. *Ch'üan T'ang shih-hua*. Shanghai: Commercial Press, 1937.

3. Other Works Consulted

BAILEY, LIBERTY HYDE. *Hortus Third: A Concise Dictionary of Plants Cultivated in the United States and Canada*. New York: Macmillan, 1976.

BARZUN, JACQUES. "History: The Muse and Her Doctors," *American Historical Review*, 77.1(February 1972), pp. 36–64.

————, and HENRY F. GRAFF. *The Modern Researcher*. New York: Harcourt Brace Jovanovich, Inc., 1977.

————. *On Writing, Editing, and Publishing*. Chicago and London: University of Chicago Press, 1971.

BLOCH, MARC. *Feudal Society*. Chicago: University of Chicago Press, 1961.

————. *French Rural History*. Berkeley: University of California Press, 1966.

————. *The Historian's Craft*. New York: Knopf, 1953.

BROOKS, E. BRUCE. "Journey Toward the West: An Asian Prosodic Embassy in the Year 1972" [Review of W. K. Wimsatt, ed., *Versification: Major Language Types*, New York: New York University Press, 1972], *HJAS*, 35(1975), pp. 221–74.

CHAN, WING-TSIT. *A Source Book of Chinese Philosophy*. Princeton: Princeton University Press, 1969.

CHANG, CARSUN. *The Development of Neo-Confucian Thought*. London: Vision Press, 1958.

CHANG, CH'ANG. *Wu-chung jen-wu chih* [A Record of People from Wu]. Taipei: Hsüeh-sheng shu-chü, 1969.

CHANG HSIANG. *Shih-tz'u-ch'ü yü-tz'u hui-shih*. Hong Kong: Chung-hua shu-chü, 1962.

CHAO YEH. *Wu Yüeh ch'un-ch'iu (SPTK)*.

CHAO YUEN REN. "Popular Chinese Plant Words: A Descriptive Lexico-Grammatical Study," *Language*, 29(1953), pp. 379–414.

CHAVANNES, EDOUARD. "Le Royaume de Wou et de Yue," *TP*, 17 (1916), pp. 129–264.

CHAVES, JONATHAN. *Mei Yao-ch'en and the Development of Early Sung Poetry*. New York and London: Columbia University Press, 1976.

CHEN SHIH-HSIANG. "The *Shih-ching*: Its Generic Significance in Chinese Literary History and Poetics," in *Studies in Chinese Literary Genres*, Cyril Birch, ed. Berkeley: University of California Press, 1974, pp. 8–41.

CHENG CHEN-TO. *Chung-kuo wen-hsüeh ch'a-t'u shih.* 4 vols. Hong Kong: Ku-wen shu-chü, n.d.

CHENG CHI-HSIEN. "Analyse du langage poétique dans la poésie chinoise classique," *Tel Quel,* 48/49(Spring 1972), pp. 33–46.

―――. *Analyse formelle de l'oeuvre poétique d'un auteur des T'ang, Zhang Ruo-xu.* Paris and The Hague: Mouton, 1970.

CH'IEN YEN, compiler. *Wu-Yüeh pei-shih. (Hsüeh-chin t'ao-yüan* ed.).

CHING, JULIA. "Neo-Confucian Utopia Theories and Political Ethics," *Monumenta Serica,* 30(1972–73), pp. 1–56.

CHI-LIN TA-HSÜEH CHUNG-WEN-HSI [Chinese Department of Chi-lin University]. *Chung-kuo wen-hsüeh shih-kao.* 4 vols. Ch'ang-ch'un: Chi-lin jen-min ch'u-pan-she, 1961.

CHUNG-KUO WEN-HSÜEH-SHIH PIEN-HSIEH-TSU [Editorial Group for a History of Chinese Literature]. *Chung-kuo wen-hsüeh shih* [History of Chinese Literature]. Peking: Jen-min ch'u-pan-she, 1963.

DAVIS, A. R. "The Double Ninth Festival in Chinese Poetry: A Study of Variations Upon a Theme," in *Wen-lin,* pp. 45–64.

DEBON, GÜNTHER. "Some Aspects and Structures of the Chinese Poem," *Tamkang Review,* 6.2 (October 1975) and 7.1 [combined issue](April 1976), pp. 127–42.

DOWNER, G. B. and A. C. GRAHAM. "Tone Patterns in Chinese Poetry," *BSOAS,* 1963, pp. 145–48.

EBERHARD, WOLFRAM. *Conquerors and Rulers: Social Forces in Medieval China.* 2nd ed.; Leiden: E. J. Brill, 1965.

EDWARDS, E. D. "A Classified Guide to the Thirteen Classes of Chinese Prose," *BSOAS,* 12(1947–48), pp. 770–88.

EICHHORN, WERNER. "Ursachen, Gegner und Anfänge des Neu-Konfuzianismus," *Sinica,* 16(1941), pp. 34–47.

ELVIN, MARK. *The Pattern of the Chinese Past.* Stanford: Stanford University Press, 1973.

ERIKSON, ERIK H. *Young Man Luther.* New York: Norton, 1958.

EVANS, RICHARD L. *Dialogue with Erik Erikson.* New York: E. P. Dutton, 1969.

FRANKE, HERBERT. "Some Random Notes on Fact and Fancy in Chinese History," *OE,* 22.1(June 1975), pp. 1–10.

FRANKE, OTTO. *Geschichte des chinesischen Reiches.* 5 vols. Reprint; Taipei: Ch'eng-wen Publishing Company, 1967.

FRANKEL, HANS H. *The Flowering Plum and the Palace Lady.* New Haven: Yale University Press, 1976.

FUNG YU-LAN. "The Rise of Neo-Confucianism and its Borrowing from Buddhism and Taoism," *HJAS,* 7(1942), pp. 89–125.

GARDNER, JOHN. *The Life and Times of Chaucer.* New York: Alfred A. Knopf, 1972.

GERNET, JACQUES. *Le Monde chinois*. Paris: Cobin, 1972.

GRIMAUD, MICHEL. "Recent Trends in Psychoanalysis: A Survey with Emphasis on Psychological Criticism in English Literature and Related Areas," *Substance*, 13(1976), pp. 136–62.

HARRISON, JAMES. *The Communists and Chinese Peasant Rebellions*. New York: Antheneum, 1969.

HAWKES, DAVID. *Ch'u Tz'u, the Songs of the South*. Oxford: Clarendon Press, 1959.

HERS, J. "Chinese Names of Plants, A Preliminary List of the Trees and Shrubs of North Honan," *Journal of the North China Branch, Royal Asiatic Society*, 53(1922), pp. 105–17.

HOU WAI-LU. *Chung-kuo ssu-hsiang t'ung-shih*. Peking: Jen-min ch'u-pan-she, 1960.

Hsiang-yang hsien-chih. 3 vols. in *Hu-pei fang-chih*. Taipei: Taiwan hsüeh-sheng shu-chü, 1969.

HSIAO KUNG-CH'ÜAN. *Chung-kuo cheng-chih ssu-hsiang shih*. Taipei: Chung-hua wen-hua ch'u-pan shih-yeh wei-yüan hui, 1961.

JAO TSUNG-I. "Wu-Yüeh wen-hua," *CYYY*, 41.4(February 1969), pp. 609–39.

KUO MAO-CH'IEN. *Yüeh-fu shih-chi. (SPPY)*.

LAU, D. C., translator. *Mencius*. Baltimore: Penguin, 1970.

————. "Translating Philosophical Works in Classical Chinese—Some Difficulties," in *The Art and Profession of Translation*, T. C. Lai, editor. Hong Kong: Hong Kong Translation Society, 1977, pp. 52–60.

LI, H. L. *The Garden Flowers of China*. New York: Ronald Press, 1959.

LIU HSIEH. *The Literary Mind and the Carving of Dragons*. Vincent Yu-chung Shih, translator. Taipei: Chung-hua Book Co., 1970.

LIU PO-CHI. *T'ang-tai cheng-chiao shih*. Taipei: Chung-hua shu-chü, 1974.

LIU TA-CHIEH. *Chung-kuo wen-hsüeh fa-chan shih*. 2 vols. Peking: Chung-hua shu-chü, 1973 and 1977.

————. "T'ang-tai she-hui yü wen-hsüeh ti fa-chan" [The Development of T'ang Society and Literature], *Xuexi yu pipan*, 1975.8, pp. 41–50.

LO, IRVING YUCHENG. "Fidelity in Translation and the Limits of Uncivility," in *The Art and Profession of Translation*, pp. 107–22.

————., and WU-CHI LIU, editors. *Sunflower Splendor*. New York: Doubleday/Anchor, 1975.

LO KEN-TSE. *Chung-kuo wen-hsüeh p'i-p'ing shih*. 3 vols. Peking: Ku-tien wen-hsüeh ch'u-pan-she, 1957.

LU KAN-JU and FENG YÜAN-CHÜN. *Chung-kuo shih-shih* [A History of Chinese Poetry]. 3 vols. Hong Kong: Ku-wen shu-chü, 1968.

MA TUAN-LIN, compiler. *Wen-hsien t'ung-k'ao*. Shanghai: Commercial Press, 1935 *(Shih-t'ung* ed.).

MA TSUNG-HUO. *Chung-kuo ching-hsüeh-shih*. 3 vols. Shanghai: Commercial Press, 1937.

MASPERO, HENRI and ETIENNE BALAZS. *Histoire et institutions de la Chine.* Paris: Presses Universitaires de France, 1967.

MATSUDA TOSHIO and MORI KEIZŌ, editors. *Ajia rekishi chizu* [Historical Atlas of Asia]. Tokyo: Heibonsha, 1966.

MERTON, ROBERT. *Social Theory and Social Structure.* New York: Free Press, 1968.

METZGER, THOMAS A. "Chinese Bandits: The Traditional Perceptions Reevaluated," *JAS*, 33.3(May 1974), pp. 455–58.

MIAO, RONALD C. "On the Translation of Traditional Chinese Poetry: A Review of Some Recent Trends," *YCGL*, 24(1975), pp. 93–103.

MURAMATSU, YŪJI. "Some Themes in Chinese Rebel Ideologies," in *Confucian Persuasion.* Stanford: Stanford University Press, 1960, pp. 241–67.

NIENHAUSER, WILLIAM H., JR. "Diction, Dictionaries and the Translation of Classical Chinese Poetry," *TP*, 64(1978), pp. 1–63.

NISBET, ROBERT A. *Tradition and Revolt, Historical and Sociological Essays.* New York: Random House, 1968.

OWEN, STEPHEN. "The Limits of Translation," *YCGL*, 24(1975), pp. 83–93.

PREMINGER, ALEX, editor. *Princeton Encyclopedia of Poetry and Poetics.* Princeton: Princeton University Press, 1972.

PRUŠEK, JAROSLAV and ZBIGNIEW SLUPSKI, editors. *Dictionary of Oriental Literatures.* Vol. 1 East Asia. 3 vols. London: Allen and Unwin, 1974.

RICKETT, ADELE A. "The Personality of the Chinese Critic," in *The Personality of the Critic,* Joseph P. Strelka, editor. University Park: Penn State University Press, 1973, pp. 111–34.

SAEKI TOMI. *Chūgoku zuihitsu zatcho sakuin.* Kyoto: Kyōtō daigaku tōyōshi kenkyūkai, 1960.

SCHOLES, ROBERT. *Structuralism in Literature.* New Haven: Yale University Press, 1974.

SHEEHY, GAIL. *Passages, Predictable Crises of Adult Life.* New York: E. P. Dutton, 1976.

SHIH, VINCENT YU-CHUNG. "Some Chinese Rebel Ideologies," *TP*, 44(1956), pp. 150–266.

SOOTHILL, WILLIAM EDWARD. *A Dictionary of Chinese Buddhist Terms.* London: Kegan Paul, Trench, Trubner and Co., 1957.

SUN KUANG-HSIEN (d. 968). *Pei meng so-yen.* [*Ya-yü-t'ang ts'ung-shu* ed.].

TU YA-CH'ÜAN. *Chih-wu-hsüeh ta tz'u-tien* (A Dictionary of Botanical Terms). 2 vols. Taipei: Wen-kuang t'u-shu yu-hsien kung-ssu, 1971.

WAKEMAN, FREDERICK, JR. "Rebellion and Revolution: The Study of Popular Movements in Chinese History," *JAS*, 36.2(February 1977), pp. 201–37.

WALLS, JAN W. "The Craft of Translating Poetic Structures and Patterns: Fidelity to Form," *YCGL*, 24(1975), pp. 68–75.

WANG AN-SHIH (1021–1086), compiler. *Wang Ching-kung T'ang pai-chia shih-hsüan.* Shanghai: Tung-fang shu-chü, 1935.

WANG, C. H. *The Bell and the Drum. A Study of the Shih Ching as Formulaic Poetry.* Berkeley: University of California Press, 1974.

WANG, JOHN C. "M. H. Abrams' Four Artistic Coordinates and Fiction Criticism in Traditional China," *Literature East and West,* 16(1972), pp. 997–1012.

WANG LI. *Han-yü shih-lü hsüeh.* Hong Kong: Chung-hua shu-chü, 1973.

Wen-yüan ying-hua. 10 vols. Taipei: Hua-wen shu-chü, 1965.

WICKERT-MICKNAT, GISELA. "Dichtung als historische Quelle," *Saeculum,* 21(1970), pp. 57–70.

WONG KAI CHEE. "Li-hsüeh-chia chih wen-i ssu-hsiang shih-lun" (A Preliminary Discussion of the Literary Thought of the Neo-Confucians), *Chung Chi Journal,* 7.2(May 1968), pp. 187–96.

WU CHING-HSÜ. *Li-tai shih-hua.* 3 vols. Taipei: Shih-chieh shu-chü, 1961.

YIN CHU. *Ho-nan hsien-sheng wen-chi. (SPPY).*

YÜ YING-SHIH. "Life and Immortality in the Mind of the Han Chinese," *HJAS,* 25(1964–65), pp. 80–122.

VON ZACH, ERWIN, translator. *Han Yü's Poetische Werke.* Cambridge, Mass.: Harvard University Press, 1952.

Finding List of Translations
of P'i Jih-Hsiu's Works in this Volume

The left-hand column lists the page numbers on which the translation is found; the center column, the translated title of the work; and the right-hand column, the location of the original (*chüan* and page) in volume 9 of the *Ch'üan T'ang-shih* [*Shih*] (Taipei: Ming-lun ch'u-pan-she, 1971) or volume 17 of the *Ch'üan T'ang-wen* [*Wen*] (Taipei: Wen-yu shu-tien, 1972).

Index

Abrams, M. H., 38
acorns, 79–80
Analects of Confucius (Lun-yü), 24, 53, 55, 56, 99
analogy *(pi)*, 46
ancient-style verse, see old-style verse
Anhwei, 13, 27
Apricot Garden, The, 29, 36
Arab traders, 18
Art of Chinese Poetry, The, by James J. Y. Liu, 38
axes of Ying, the, 48

Bailey, Liberty Hyde, 10
Balazs, Etienne, 9
Belle Lodging Palace (Kuan-wa Kung), 86, 87
Book of Changes (I-ching), 24, 45, 56; "Hsi-tz'u" section, 45
Book of Documents (Shu-ching), 24, 75
Book of Filial Obedience (Hsiao-ching), 24
Book of Poetry (Shih-ching), 24, 40, 74; Mao Commentary to, 40; quotation illustrating parallelism in, 47; "Shih jen" (The Stately Lady), 97
Book of Rites (Li-chi), 19, 24
Buddhism, 68; criticism of, 57, 59; customs of, 63; oral proselytization, 20, 64; temples, 60

"Canon of Shun" *(Book of Documents)*, cited, 50
"Canon of Yao" *(Book of Documents)*, cited, 47
Canton, 98

cassia tree, 94, 95, 134, n.73
Ch'an-shu (Book of Slander) by Lo Yin, 29
Ch'ang-an, 13, 17, 26, 27, 30, 32, 33, 34, 81
Chang An-shih (d. 62 B.C.), 28
Chang Chi (766–829), 21; his school of late-T'ang poetry, 69
Chang Ch'i-wen, 111
Chang Chih-ho *(ca, 730-ca. 810)*, 78
Ch'ang-chou (Wu-chin County, Kiangsu), 13, 32
Chang Hu, 42
Chang Hua (232–300), 107
Chang Pen, 106, 107, 108
Chao Tun, 66
Ch'ao Kung-wu (d. 1171), 110
Chekiang, 78
Ch'en Chen-sun *(ca.* 1190–1249), 110
Cheng Ch'eng (prefect of Ying-chou), 26
Cheng Chu (d. 835), directs execution of Wang Shou-ch'eng, 16
Cheng Tan, 87, 89, 91, 92
Cheng Tsai-fa, 10
Cheng Yü (P'i Jih-hsiu's examiner), 29, 30, 122, n. 92
Ch'eng Yen (fl. *ca.* 900), 19
Ch'i (ancient state of), 80, 90
Ch'i dynasty (founded by Huang Ch'ao), 13, 34
Chi-lin, 107
Chia Tao (779–849), 21; his school of late-T'ang poetry, 69
Chieh (ancient emperor), 64
Chien-an (196–220) reign period, 47
Chih-wu hsüeh ta tz'u-tien (A Dictionary

DATE DUE

JUL 16 1979